Cover

When the railway was extended from Woking through to Guildford and Portsmouth it cut Oaks Farm in two. The farmer, Mr Brothers, complained that he could not get his cows from one part of his farm to the other, so a bridge was built, or rather two bridges. Oaks Farm became part of the parish of St Mary of Bethany church. The parish straddled the railway, hence the title of this book.

For some years, from 1947, the sketch was used on the cover of St Mary of Bethany church magazine when it was called 'Twin Bridges'. It was later used with this book's title for the news page.

The sketch was drawn by Mr Walter Heath of Star Hill who had moved to Chelsea by the time the first issue was published.

Richard Lower

Both Sides Of The Bridges

The Story of
St Mary of Bethany Parish Church
Woking

1907-2007

Richard Langtree

Published by Richard Langtree

Printed and bound by The Knaphill Print Co Ltd

ISBN 978–0–9557748–0–5

It is a great privilege for me to be invited to contribute this Foreword. The account of how St Mary of Bethany church in Woking came to be built I have always found deeply moving. Richard Langtree has carefully researched the life and ministry of William Hamilton and explained how out of bereavement and tragedy came the generous gift of a memorial church. Janet, my wife, developed a special affection for the east window depicting three scenes from the life of Mary of Bethany, as described in the Gospels.

Now there is a second story to be told. This is the account of the ministry of the Church's clergy and people over the last one hundred years. Having been opened for worship in 1907, it became a parish church in 1923, and the first Vicar was appointed in 1924. I was the fourth Vicar, but I came to Woking when my three predecessors were still living, and many folk were around who remembered William Hamilton and told me about him. In 1973 I came from Liverpool to preach on the occasion of the 50th anniversary of the formation of the parish.

During my time in Woking St Mary of Bethany was the home church of a number of men and women serving overseas with missionary societies, and also for several young men who heard God's call to ordained ministry. A number of families moved on to other parts of the country, and told me they would look for another church with a similar warmth of welcome, the same clear message of the Gospel, and the same commitment to supporting Christian work elsewhere. That was our reputation, I pray that it will always be so.

Raymond J Lee
Vicar of St Mary of Bethany
1962-1970
Canon Emeritus of Liverpool Cathedral

St Mary of Bethany has been 'my' church almost from the day I was born. My father Frank, grandfather John and great uncle Harry were also members of St Mary's and of the choir.

I thought about writing a centenary history about four years ago. This was a completely new venture as I had not done undertaken any research before. Like family history it is absorbing and time consuming. It seems to have no end which made publishing this book difficult. You have to stop when there is a deadline. Therefore there may be inaccuracies and omissions for which I apologise. I would be pleased to receive any further information via St Mary of Bethany church office. I have tried to acknowledge any copy or photographs where the copyright holder is known.

Although I have listed acknowledgements at the back of the book I would like to especially thank Rev Raymond Lee for his interest in St Mary's history when he was vicar here and my wife Gill for her patience.

Richard Langtree 2007

Contents

Part I
Introduction

"Acres and acres of golden corn once waved over the whole area where the church of St Mary of Bethany now stands."

A charming drawing of St Marys which was used for the front cover of the magazine and Christmas cards around 1960. This shows the west entrance and porch added in 1956 before the Hamilton Memorial Hall was built. The original entrance was just to the right of the buttress.

Artist
Ruth Goldney.

Woking is a 'new' town 25 miles to the south west of London in the county of Surrey. It is on the railway line from London Waterloo to the south and west of England. 'New' Woking grew after the railway was built across common land to the north of 'old' Woking and an urgent need for extra burial space was required for London.

St Mary of Bethany church is a Church of England Anglican parish church, one of 15 in the Woking Deanery, 70 in the Dorking Archdeaconry and 162 in the Diocese of Guildford. It is situated to the west of the Woking town centre parish of Christ Church. St Mary of Bethany was built to accommodate a rapidly expanding population which resulted in 7 new churches being built around Woking in the space of 25 years. The parish was mainly taken out of Christ Church parish and to this day Christ Church is St Marys sponsor.

St Mary of Bethany church was originally in the huge diocese of Winchester but was transferred to the new diocese of Guildford when it was formed from the northern part of Winchester diocese in 1927.

St Mary of Bethany church was one of many designed by the architect W D Caröe.

With the loss of many fine buildings throughout the country a listing scheme was introduced in the Town and Country Planning Act 1971. St Mary's was designated a Grade 2 listed building on 6th January 1984.

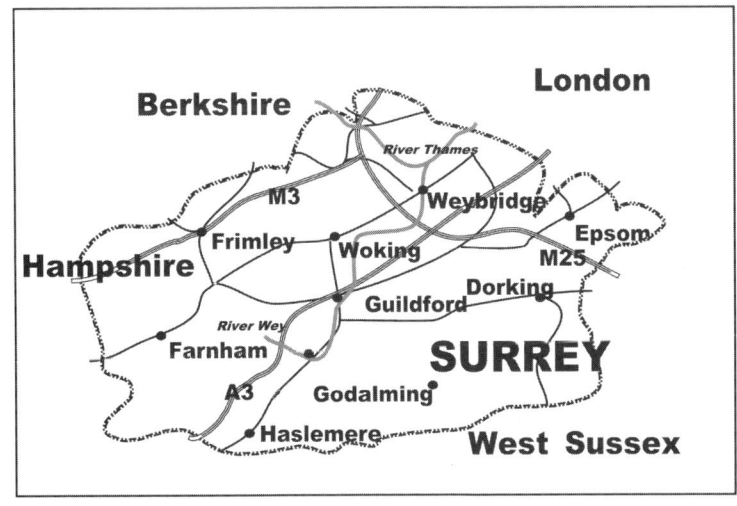

Diocese of Guildford 2007.

The development of Woking in the late 19th century was inextricably linked to the arrival of the railway. Woking up until then was the village surrounding St Peters church in what we now call Old Woking. The area to the north was mostly common land owned by the Lord of the Manor, Lord Onslow and leased out for grazing. There were a few farms and hamlets scattered around.

The Basingstoke canal had been cut in 1794 passing through the common land. It had little impact on local development except for a number of brickworks which opened to supply locally made bricks for the construction of the canal, and some nurseries which built up by it. It was built to give easier, faster and cheaper transportation of agricultural goods from Basingstoke to London; and coal, wood and manufactured goods the other way.

The London to Southampton railway opened on 21st May 1838 between Nine Elms and a temporary terminus at Woking Common. Railway fever was at its height and in the space of 21 years the line had been extended to Basingstoke 1839, Southampton 1840, Guildford 1845 and Portsmouth 1859. However, initially even this had very little effect on development around Woking Common (as the station was then called) with the exception of The Railway Hotel (now The Sovereigns) which was built in 1840. The railway was a success though, by taking traffic from the London - Portsmouth (A3) road.

The Cholera epidemic of 1842 in London brought about rapid change. Churchyards were full, unhygienic and objectionable methods were employed to increase capacity. Londoners were worried about the 'foul' air (miasma) because they thought that cholera was spread through the air. Permission to open new cemeteries was not granted and burials were not allowed on unconsecrated ground. Parliament closed overcrowded cemeteries in 1850.

The London Necropolis and National Mausoleum Co was formed and had a bill passed in Parliament in 1852 allowing for the compulsory purchase of land outside London for burials. They chose Woking Common, owing to easy railway access, cheap land and sandy soil and so bought over 2000 acres of land from the Lord of the Manor, Lord Onslow. Brookwood Cemetery was opened in 1854. Whether all the land was ever required for burials or a profit could be seen in reselling the land is not clear. But later another bill was passed to enable the L N & N M Co to sell common land for development. In the end only 400 acres was kept as Brookwood Cemetery. The Necropolis Co started to sell

land in large plots to the south of the railway. 41 acres were purchased by John Rastrick for a family house adjacent to the south side of the station effectively barring development of Woking to the south, which would have been the logical direction. Local government ineptitude did not help. Woking's local authority at the time being Guildford which, for one thing, did not want another town built too close to Guildford competing for trade.

To the north of the railway smaller plots were sold and thus Woking came into being around 1870. Houses were built along the High Street which were soon converted into shops. Woking very quickly developed in the space of 40 years with many large institutions taking the opportunity to build on low priced land:-

1859 Invalid Convict Prison
1862 Royal Dramatic College
1867 Surrey County Asylum for Pauper Lunatics
1879 Crematorium, the first one in the country
1885 St Peter's Memorial Home
1889 Shah Jehan Mosque
1893 St Peters Convent
1909 London & South Western Railway
            Servant's Orphanage

Large institutions made use of cheap land.

Other buildings and services found in any town were also established:-

1856 The Albion Hotel
1869 The Red House Hotel
1872 First Church (Weslyan Chapel)
1874 School (Board School Road)
1877 Christ Church (the original 'Iron Room')
1882 Mains Water
1887 Police Station
1890 Mains Electricity
1892 Mains Gas
1895 Woking Urban District Council formed
1895 Fire Brigade
1895 Street Lighting
1899 Victoria Hospital
1899 Mains Sewerage

Growth of Woking's buidings and services.

To the south of the town larger properties were built mostly on land sold by farmers which was not owned by the Necropolis Co. The York Estate was built both sides of York Road between Guildford Road and the Twin Bridges. The West Hill Park Estate was bounded by the railway to the north,

the footpath at the Twin Bridges to the east, Whitstreet Lane (Wych Hill) to the west and Guildford Road to the south. The York Estate was deemed to be inferior to Mount Hermon owing to its proximity to the railway. To the east of Guildford Road the 'Hillview Estate' was developed in the late 1880s and early '90s by the Suburban Land Company, who gave part of their land to Woking Council to lay out the 'Mount Hermon Recreation Ground' - now known as 'Woking Park'.

Because of its close proximity to the town and station, much of this area was redeveloped in the 1950s and 60s as high-density housing. Many of the Victorian properties have been demolished to make way for flats and houses, but in the West Hill Road area the 'Mount Hermon Conservation Area' has helped to preserve some of the former Victorian and Edwardian splendour.

This is a very brief history of the beginning of Woking to set the scene. Continuing in the same vein is the story of the development of Woking's churches (Church of England).

Taken from Elsie Wright's unpublished history of St Mary of Bethany.

"Acres and acres of golden corn once waved over the whole area where the church of St Mary of Bethany now stands. This great cornfield stretched from the railway to Guildford Road and from the footpath in Mount Hermon Road to Wych Hill Lane. It belonged to a farmer named Brothers, whose farmhouse 'Oak Farm' was in Goldsworth Road near the footpath. A continuation of this footpath over the Tin Bridges skirted the cornfield down to a stile leading onto Guildford Road near the round-about. Just a narrow field path beneath a hedgerow. It was an ancient church footpath leading in both directions to a Parish Church - Saint Peter's Woking, and Saint Marys Horsell. A coin of Charles II's reign has been unearthed - somebody's collection perhaps. In 1838 when the railway had come, cutting through the farmland, farmers complained that their 'cow walk' was gone, and so the Tin Bridges were built to accommodate the cows. Coming back to within living memory, across what was then the end of Mount Hermon Road stood a thick hedge with a wee gap through which one went into the cornfield".

Woking was growing. The railway was starting to have a huge effect on the town and the population grew very quickly in the late 1890's.

Rev William Hamilton had moved from St Johns to Woking in 1893 to be first vicar of the new town centre church, Christ Church, and he could see his parish population increasing and his work load was apparently too high. You can see from the table below the very large population increase in the twenty years between 1891 and 1911. The population rose from 12612 to 28747. Hence the requirement for splitting the parish. All Saints Woodham was opened in 1893 to the east of Woking. William Hamilton was instrumental in raising funds for the building of   St Pauls as a chapel of ease in 1895 to the east of the town in Oriental Road. Then St Mary of Bethany - 1907 to the west of the town. To the north of the town St Mary the Virgin Horsell had been serving the small population of Horsell for centuries but even that had been subject to Victorian   alterations partly to   accommodate the increasing population and to satisfy the Victorian fashion of 'improvement'. St Peter's church had also been serving the people in the original Woking - Old Woking to the south - for centuries.

Woking settled down to steady growth until the early 1950s when it saw exceptional growth again due to the building of local authority estates at, amongst other locations, Sheerwater Valley and Barnsbury Farm. Barnsbury became part of St Mary of Bethany parish in 1975.   The building of new dwellings culminated with the building of Goldsworth Park, reputed to be the largest private development of its kind in Europe at the time, necessitating another new parish; St Andrews. In 1999-2004 more housing was built on the site of the old Brookwood Hospital.

Census Year	Pop.	Growth
1801	2,425	
1851	4,651	2,226
1861	5,758	1,107
1871	8,755	2,997
1881	11,058	2,303
1891	12,612	1,554
1901	20,565	7,953
1911	28,747	8,182
1921	31,755	3,008
1931	36,151	4,396
1941	43,500*	5,849
1951	47,596	5,596
1961	67,519	19,923
1971	76,842	9,323
1981	81,800	9,938
1991	84,400	2,600
2001	89,836	5,436

Woking population Growth.

* This is an estimated figure. There was no Census taken during the 2nd World War.

Both Sides
Of The Bridge

No story of Woking would be complete without a picture of Christ Church. Rev WFT Hamilton raised the money to build it while he was vicar of St Johns.
This rare drawing was published in The Building News 1892.

The first date is the dedication of a chapel-of-ease or consecration of a parish church building. The parish and second date show when a new parish was created and from which existing parish it was mostly formed.

The population of the area we know as Woking Borough (as distinct from ecclesiastical Parish boundaries) was increasing rapidly. The requirement for churches in the late 1890's was as great as any other building and new churches sprung up to accommodate the increasing population and its spread away from the town centre. As new churches were established parish sizes began to reduce in area. At that time the Woking area was in the Winchester Diocese and its parishes for centuries had been Horsell, (Old) Woking, Byfleet and Pyrford. Between 1842 and 1909 the number of new churches and parishes had multiplied to include:

THE BUILDING NEWS, MAY. 27. 1892.

CHRIST-CHURCH·WOKING   S·E· VIEW

W.F. UNSWORTH. FRIBA· ARCHT.

St John the Baptist 1842
    Parish 1884 (Old Woking)
Christ Church 1893
    Parish 1893 (Old Woking)
All Saints Woodham 1894
    Parish 1902 (Addlestone and Horsell)
St Pauls Maybury 1895
    Parish 1958 (Christ Church)
St Mary of Bethany 1907
    Parish 1923 (Christ Church)
Holy Trinity Knaphill 1907
    Parish 1907
St Saviours Brookwood 1909
    Chapel of Ease to Holy Trinity Knaphill

Woking owes much to William Hamilton; his vision of a rapidly expanding town and therefore the need for churches in the growth areas. William Frederick Tucker Hamilton was born in 1856 in London, the third of four children. He was the son of Otho William Hawtrey Hamilton a civil servant and Dorothea Laura Hamilton née Tucker. He was educated at Malvern and then at Trinity College Cambridge where he was a prominent member of the Daily Prayer Meeting and a co founder, in 1877, of the Cambridge Inter-Collegiate Christian Union, known as CICCU. He was was ordained a deacon and became a curate at Holy Trinity Ripon in 1880. In 1881 he was ordained a priest and on 15th October 1881

William married Maud Stanley, daughter of Charles Stanley, a stockbroker, of Lancaster Gate, London. The following year he moved with his wife to Eastbourne where he was curate of Holy Trinity until 1886 when they moved to Woking where William became vicar of St John the Baptist church, St Johns. They were to have two children, a

Rev WFT Hamilton 1856 - 1944.

daughter Constance Maud born in 1886, followed in 1892 by a son Herbert Otho.

William restarted a building fund for a new church in Woking town centre to replace a leaking "iron room" built in 1877. He raised the capital in two years. On completion he moved there to become the first Vicar of Christ Church in 1893. William work tirelessly and with great persuasion to raise money to build Christ Church, a hall, a number of mission halls, a vicarage and also St Paul's church. In 1896 he used his own funds and purchased two plots of land from the West Hill Park Estate in Mount Hermon Road opposite

West Hill Road. 1896 plans of the land sales show that originally William Hamilton was going to purchase plots 51 and 52 - Nos 35 and 37 Mount Hermon Road. By 1899 the time of the second phase of plot sales the purchased plots had moved to plots 49 and 51 opposite the top of West Hill Road. At that time William also purchased plot 112 in York Road as well as a plot in the Kingsway. York Road in this second phase of sales was named New Road.

The 1841 tithe map shows that the majority of land in the West Hill Park Estate was owned by The Honourable Peter John Locke King MP, a large land owner. The land was farmed by Eldred Nunns. A smaller part along Triggs Lane was owned and farmed by William Trigg. The arable field on which St Mary of Bethany church is built belonged to Locke King, no 466 'Wych Street Six Acres'. Peter Locke King died in 1885 leaving the majority of his £500,000 (today value £28 million) estate to his son Hugh who went on to build Brooklands race track. Hugh's attitude to his landed inheritance was to sell it to finance other profitable enterprises.

When William told the seller he intended to build a church there was some discussion as to the suitability of having a church in what was to be residential area. William Hamilton in his usual persuasive manner assured the seller that a church would be a positive asset to the area.

Maud Hamilton died in 1900 aged 38 after a long illness, just after William was struck down with a stroke which he put down to the work involved in running such a large parish.

Plan showing plot nos referred to in text.

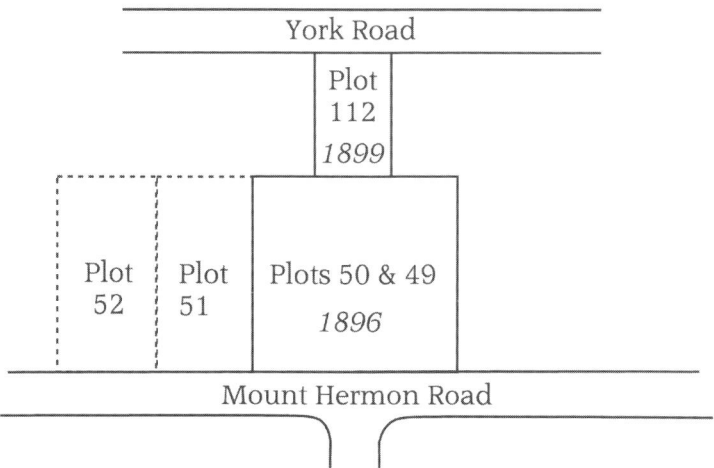

When he was offered the parish of Cromer in Norfolk in 1905 William gave the land he had bought in Mount Hermon Road, excluding the York Road end, and the cost of building a church to Christ Church.

Building a new church, at that time called church extension, necessitated an investigation by the church commissioners. This looked at the necessity for a new church, the present and future population, the siting of the building etc. The commissioners agreed to William Hamilton's proposal.

The Christ Church Parochial Church Council, and congregation were concerned that taking the new church from Christ Church would be as though the 'jam had been taken from the bread and butter', taking the wealthy members of the congregation away, but they also agreed with the proposal.

My dear churchwardens,

Last autumn, when I was feeling that the burden of this parish was becoming too great for me, I resolved in my mind plans for its division, and came to the conclusion that the most natural and satisfactory plan would be to cut off Mount Hermon and Goldsworth, and form the district west of the Guildford Road and Percy Street into a new parish...

One day the thought came into my mind that on October 15th, 1906, had my beloved wife been spared to me, we should have celebrated our silver wedding, another thought followed, that it would be sweet to erect a church to her memory, to be opened on that anniversary.

My intention was to bring this scheme before the parish, and try to raise the funds for the Vicarage. Then came, at Christmas, the offer of Cromer. It seemed to be of God that the thought of the memorial had been given me before that offer came; and when I accepted Cromer it was with the conviction that by erecting this church the great need of our parish would be met, and that, therefore, I could leave Woking with an easy mind.... ,

In February 1905 William Hamilton wrote this letter to his churchwardens.

A further tragedy was to strike the Hamilton family when in 1915 at the age of 23, Herbert was killed at the Battle of Loos in France during the Great War. William was a very dedicated family man and was distraught at the death of his wife at 38 and his son at 23 as, due to his wife's illness they had never lived together as a family of four.

William returned to Woking after his retirement in 1916 and worshipped at St Mary of Bethany church assisting with services and visiting parishioners in all three churches until November 1939, two months after the outbreak of the Second World War.

He lived, with his daughter Constance until he died on 1st November 1944 and was buried alongside his wife at St Johns churchyard after a service at St Marys. Constance moved to Eastbourne where she died in 1962 aged 76.

Part 2
Building

*"I am very fond of
simplicity, and I think
we have succeeded in
making it a real feature
of interest in this case."*
W D Caröe

William Hamilton chose W D Caröe to design St Mary of Bethany church. He was a prolific architect, producing many new churches. He was known as a master of spatial planning and a designer of striking originality. His many domestic buildings were in the 'arts and crafts' style. 'Arts and Crafts' was a reaction to flamboyant Victorian design. It was started by William Morris and later including buildings such as Caröes. The style was popular from about 1870-1920. Caröe was also a pioneer of building conservation, playing a leading role in establishing a theoretical and practical basis for the care of historical buildings.

Caröe, 1857 - 1938, the son of the consul to Denmark, went to Trinity College

W D Caröe's Summary of Reductions for reducing the cost of the building.

Cambridge and studied there at the same time as William Hamilton.

In 1895 Caröe was appointed Architect to the Ecclesiastical Commissioners. This post required him to prepare reports on specifications submitted for new parish churches which would include whether they were worthy of the parish, of appropriate size and structural soundness. He also continued to design churches himself.

Caröe not only designed the buildings but also believed that the many details and internal fittings were part of his brief including, in the case of St Mary of Bethany the choir stalls, pulpit, table, reredos, prayer desk, light fittings and even the rainwater hoppers and door latches.

By June 1905 Caröe had finished a complete set of drawings for the church in the 'Arts and Crafts' style. William Hamilton had not by then chosen a name for the church so a plan drawing showed the name as St....... Caröe's original design allowed for south and north aisles and a single storey

'lean-to' style extension on the west elevation for a baptistry, store and entrance door.

Hamilton's gift was not going to include the north or south aisles, but he did have the north aisle erected. The estimate for building the church to the original design was £5,590 0s 0d but this may not have included the south aisle because it is not mentioned in a Summary of Reductions dated November 1906. Even William Hamilton's budget would not have been unlimited and so the estimate was reduced to £4,357 4s 3d by omitting the porch and baptistry and according to the Summary of Reductions, shown here, many other items. These included omitting most of the fittings: the font, lectern, choir stalls, altar and rails, a safe, a south facing dormer window and the foundation stone. The dormer window was omitted but the other items were all included. The specification was reduced for some items including the size of the rafters and specifying Yellow Deal or Pine in lieu of Douglas Fir.

Caröe's redesign when omitting the south aisle was for the windows in the temporary wall to mirror the north aisle but this layout was not possible owing to the arches either side of the nave. Did he read his drawings incorrectly or was he going to omit the south wall arches? The clergy and choir vesteries were to be separated by a wall which was omitted but not shown on the Summary of Reductions. An "Alteration of windows" reduced the cost by the huge sum of £333 4s 11d (£333 24p), which was more than the omission of the major parts of the building. One wonders what were these alterations to windows. The diocesan architect carrying out a quinquennial inspection* of the church suggested that the west window should have stained glass installed. Perhaps this was the "Alteration of windows" - omitting the stained glass, although there is no mention in the original design for the installation of stained glass in this window.

The builder E C Hughes Ltd of Albion Works Wokingham was not appointed until 5th December 1906 a month after the laying of the foundation stone. Edmund Cecil Hughes was a Mayor and Alderman of Wokingham.

On one of the drawings there are pencilled notes of estimated costs including; font £20, vestry fittings £25, rainwater heads £3-10-0d (£3-50p) each. The floor finish, Segalith, nave red 5/6d, (27½p) nave grey 4/6d (22½p) and chancel red 6/6d (32½p), presumably per square yard.

* Quinquennial inspection. Church of England Inspection of Churches Measure 1955. This is a five-yearly inspection which is required for all churches. It is carried out by the diocesan architect to highlight maintenance work required for the building.

The date for the dedication would appear to have been moved from Oct 15th to Oct 30th, according to pencilled notes on a drawing of the choir stalls. The final date being Nov 5th.

St Mary of Bethany church is not noted as one of Caröe's best designs. Jennifer Freeman who wrote a biography of W D Caröe describes the exterior as *'weakly detailed'* but *'as more generous'* internally.

W D Caröe

During the building of St Marys Caröe stated in correspondence (not to William Hamilton) dated January 1907 that he was concurrently involved in hundreds of projects.

William Hamilton wrote to W D Caröe to thank him for designing St Marys. This reply was written on May 8th 1908.

TELEPHONE N° 5324 WESTMINSTER
TELEGRAMS "WEDECER, LONDON."

3, Great College Street,
Westminster. S.W.

My 8th., 1908.

Dear Mr. Hamilton,

Please let absence account for my delay in answering your very kind letter. I can hardly tell you what pleasure and satisfaction it gave me, as indeed has my whole connection with yourself in regard to Saint Mary of Bethany.

I am very fond of simplicity, and I think we have succeeded in making it a real feature of interest in this case; I am very glad that you think with me, and that the church will be associated in your mind with pleasure.

I hope we shall some day see the aisle and west porch complete. The laying out of the grounds adds very much to the whole effect.

W. D. Caröe

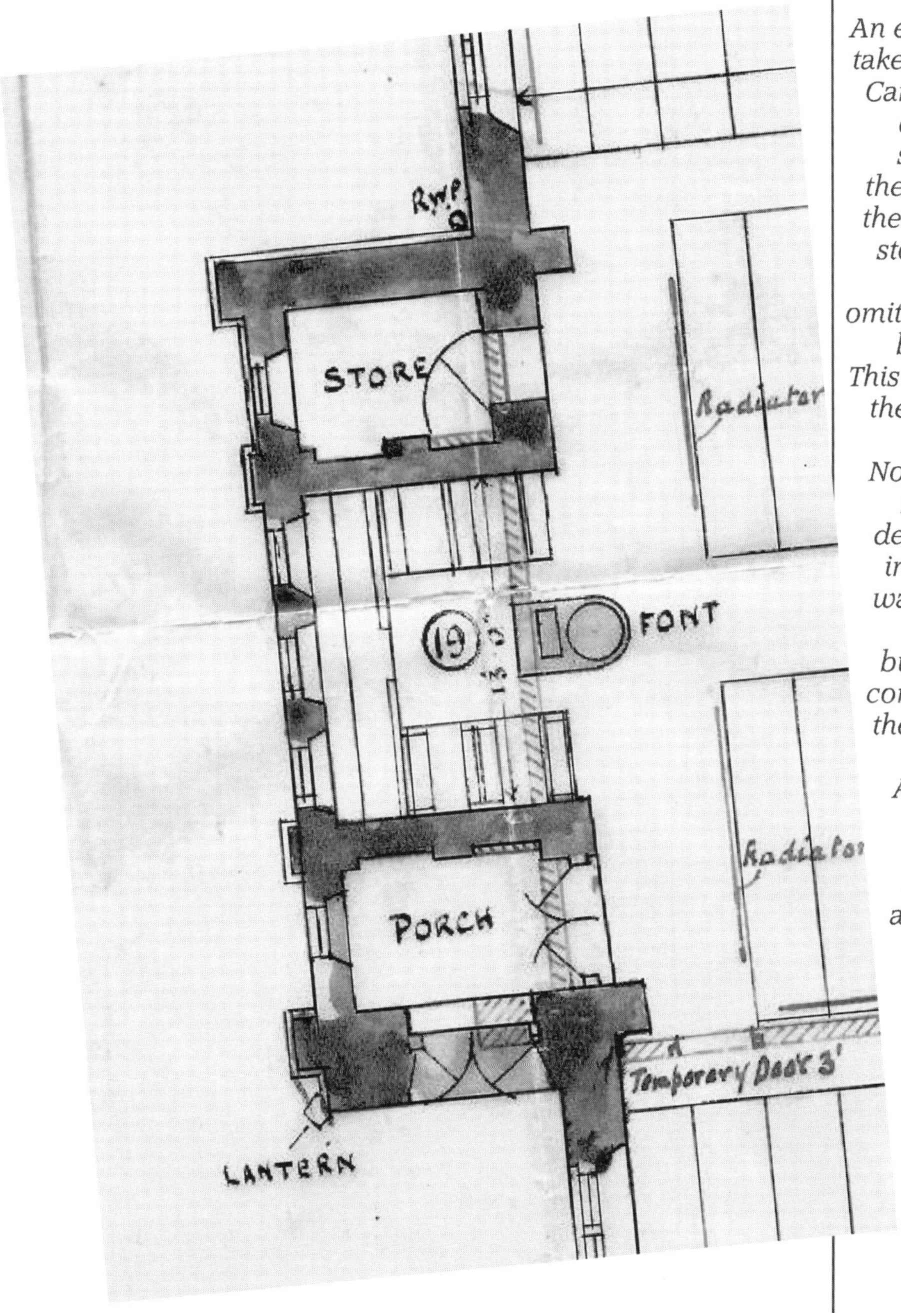

Both Sides Of The Bridges

An enlargement taken from W D Caröe's plan drawing showing the baptistry, the porch and store which were omitted from the building. This area is now the entrance lobby.
Note the red hatching denoting the insertion of walls and the enlarged buttresses to compensate for the loss of the Baptistry. Also shown are the temporary south wall and entrance door.

RWP

STORE

Radiator

19' 0"

3' 1"

FONT

PORCH

Radiator

Temporary Door 3'

LANTERN

An innovation in the building was an electric extractor fan which was built into the bell cote in 1906. It was designed to extract stale air from the highest point in the roof. The photograph above shows the extraction louvres which are not shown on any drawing.

The bell cote with the bell removed.

The Woking News and Mail report of the dedication service mentioned:-

'The interior is well ventilated, and lighted by electricity, and, with its open timber roofs and carved wood fittings, presents a spacious appearance'.

The good ventilation also included another innovation. Under some of the the windows there are ventilator grilles,

including two behind the reredos. These are connected by a flue built into the wall and terminate at grilles low down on the outside wall. These are called Tobin Tubes, named after their English inventor Martin Tobin, gentleman of Leeds, who was granted a patent in 1873. They were designed to give draught free ventilation by having sufficient length to let the air issue in a smooth vertical current without eddies. The extractor fan would presumably have assisted with drawing fresh air through the Tobin Tubes.

Martin Tobin may have invented this form of ventilation as a means to overcome the fear of cholera, tuberculosis and

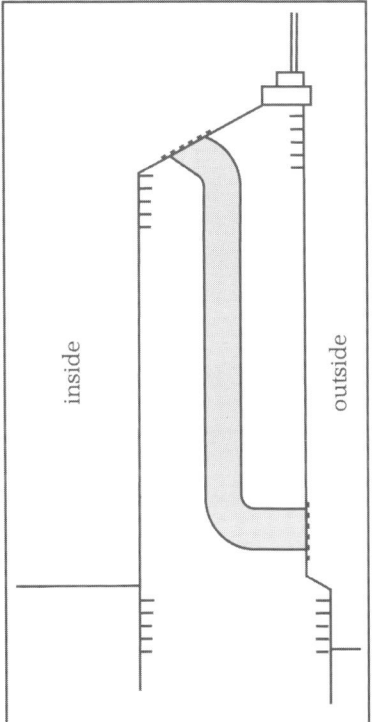

A section through the wall showing the Tobin Tubes.

other diseases spreading through the air as was thought in the 1850s.

The extractor fan is disconnected and its existence only came to light when the bell was removed for refurbishment. The external grilles for the Tobin Tubes were blanked off in 1958 after complaints about draughts but the draughts persisted. The cold air being felt was probably a convection current dropping down the window.

W D Caröe's drawing of the west and east elevations showing the south aisle and the baptistry.

The north aisle was built with the church, although it was not part of Hamilton's original offer. The south aisle and west porch/baptistry/store were never built. The south aisle, because of decreasing church attendance. The west porch, because a smaller porch was built in 1956.

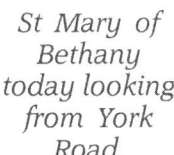

St Mary of Bethany today looking from York Road.

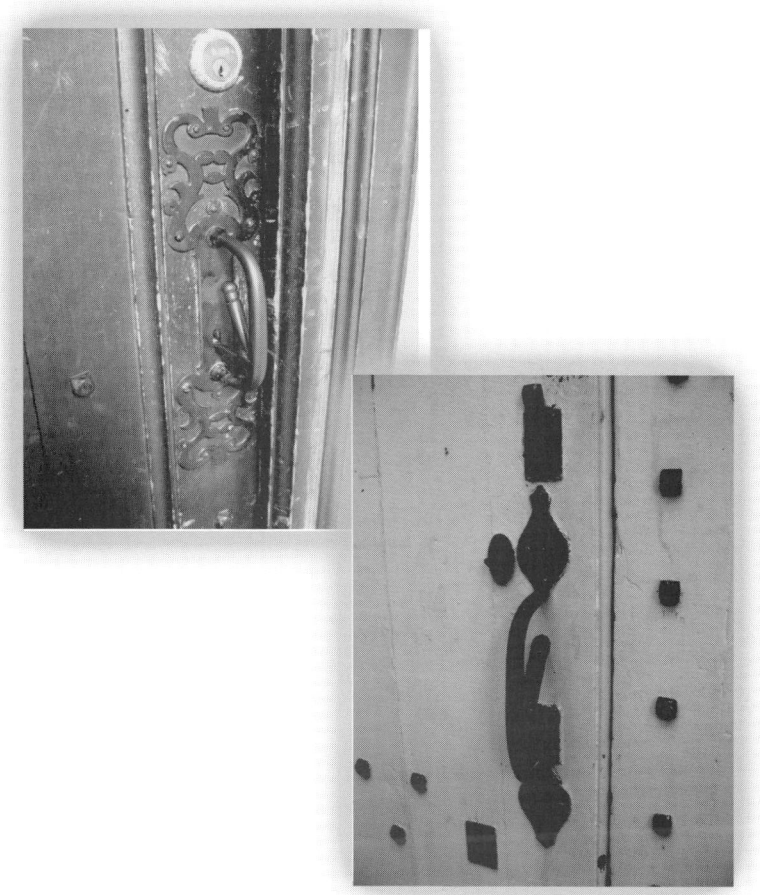

Door latches designed by Caröe.

W D Caröe designed this rainwater hopper dated 1907 and many other details.

The West Elevation as built. This is the illustration used for the front cover of the early magazines.

St Mary of Bethany, Woking.

A very early photograph of the Mount Hermon Road elevation. This is a commercial postcard postmarked 3rd July 1908. The unfinished gable is visible above the vestry door awaiting the never to be built south aisle.

Mount Hermon Road End

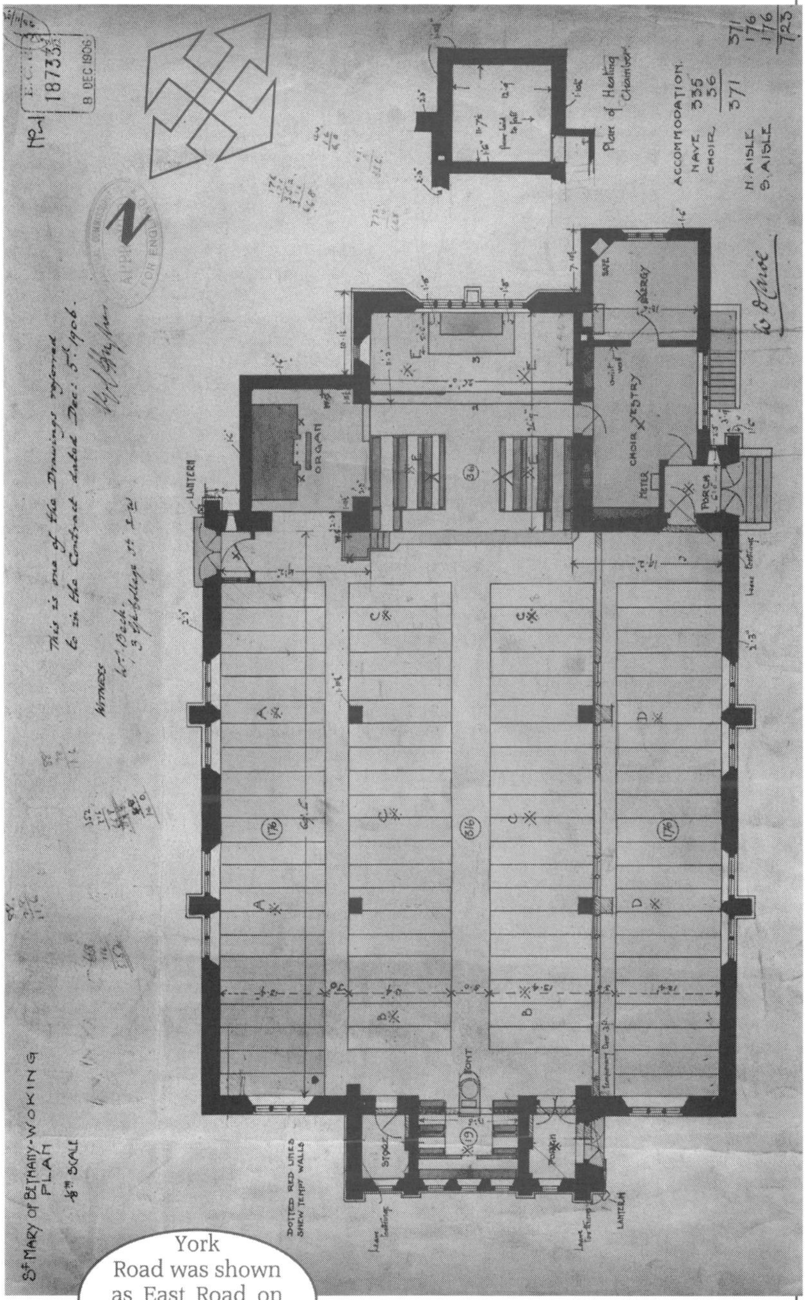

*Caröe's plan of
St Marys 1906.*

York Road was shown as East Road on Caröe's drawings of June 1905.

York Road End

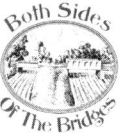

Church Plan 1959

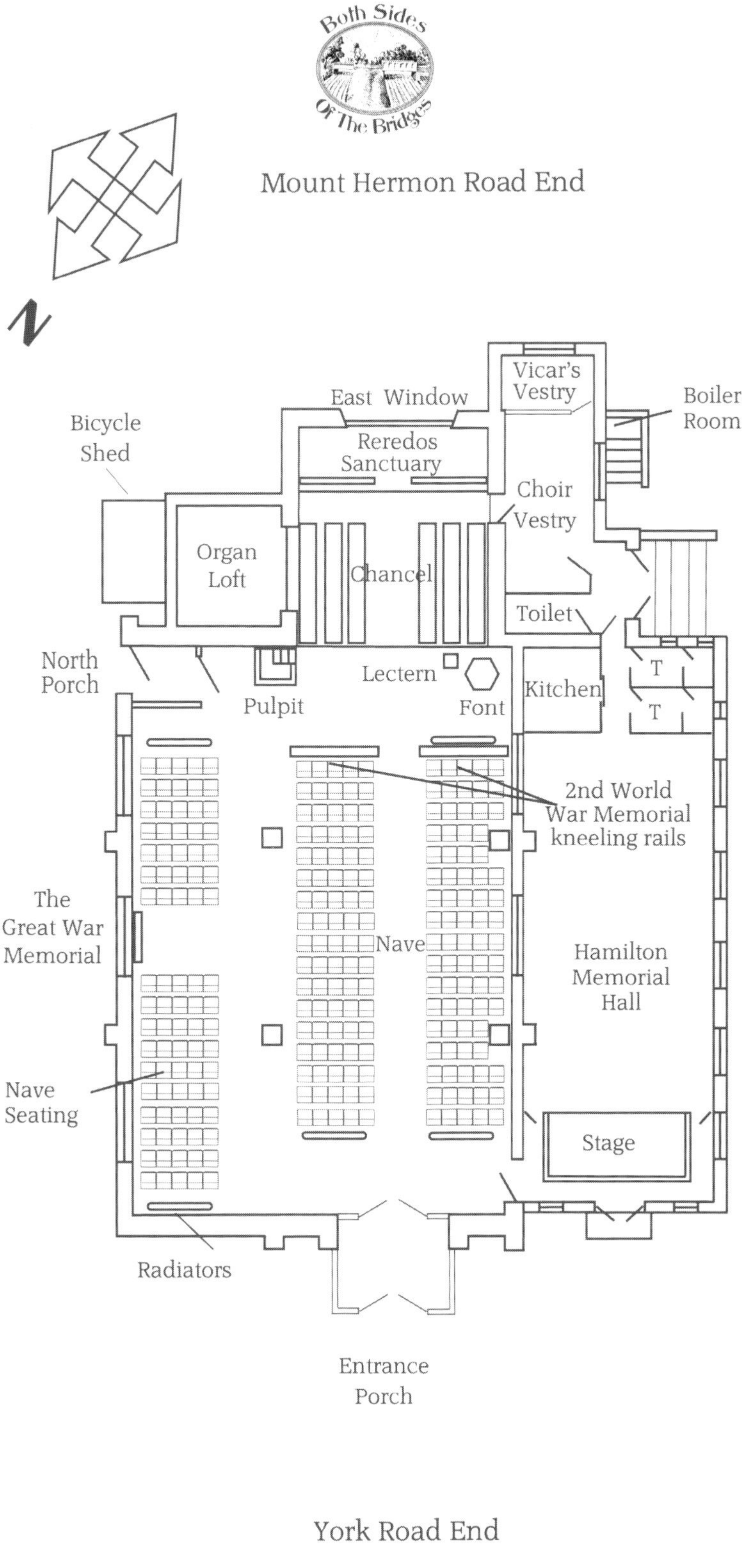

Both Sides Of The Bridges
N
Mount Hermon Road End
East Window
Vicar's Vestry
Boiler Room
Bicycle Shed
Reredos Sanctuary
Choir Vestry
Organ Loft
Chancel
Toilet
North Porch
Lectern
Kitchen
T
T
Pulpit
Font
2nd World War Memorial kneeling rails
The Great War Memorial
Nave
Hamilton Memorial Hall
Nave Seating
Stage
Radiators
Entrance Porch
York Road End

Plan of St Marys 1959.

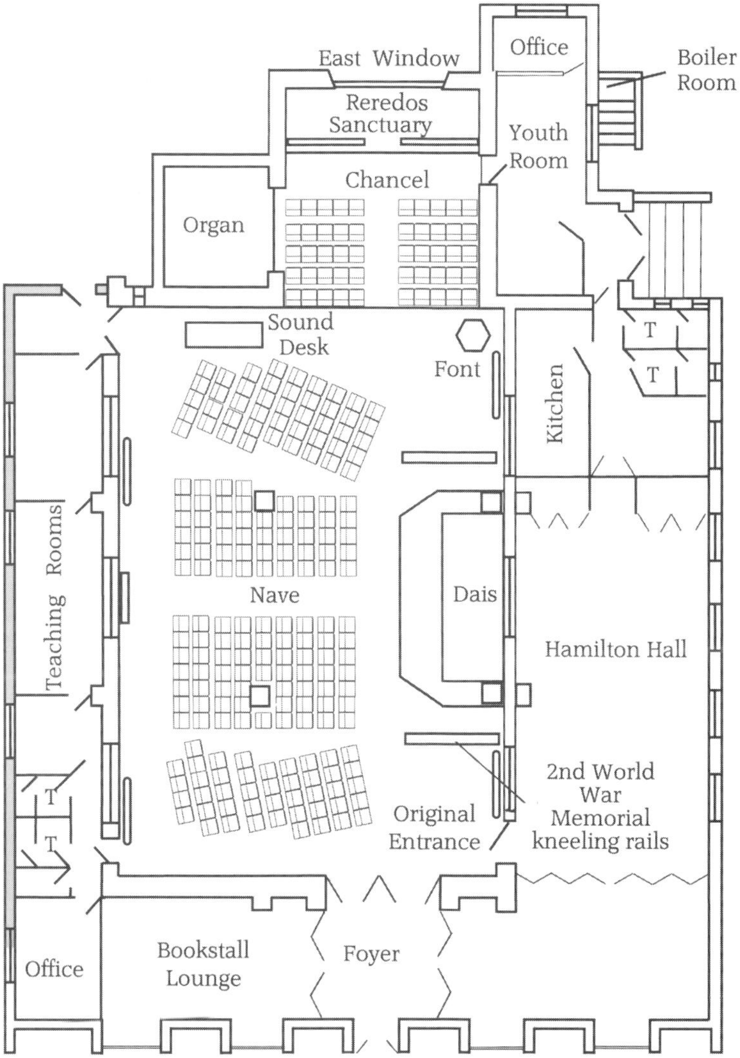

East Window

Office

Boiler
Room

Reredos
Sanctuary

Youth
Room

Chancel

Organ

Sound
Desk

Font

Kitchen

T

T

Teaching Rooms

Nave

Dais

Hamilton Hall

T

T

2nd World
War
Memorial
kneeling rails

Original
Entrance

Office

Bookstall
Lounge

Foyer

*Plan of St Marys
2007.*

Both Sides
Of The Bridges

The foundation stone is situated at the right hand side of the chancel behind the current siting of the font.

Report from the Woking News and Mail. Southwold is No. 29 Mount Hermon Road.

'The preparations for the event were made by Messers J. Harris and Son, builders, of Woking, no contract having been made for the building. Under a temporary awning, a platform had been erected, rising above which sufficient bricks had been laid to take the memorial stone. Beyond this pile there was no trace of builders handiwork on the site. The congregation assembled round the platform, upon which also some few found seats. The clergy and choir robed at Southwold, and marched in procession to the ceremony....'.

Christ Church's vicar Rev E R Price Deveraux presented William with

'a trowel and mallet, the former, an exceedingly handsome specimen of the silversmiths art, mounted with ivory handle'.

with which to perform the ceremony. William left the trowel to his daughter Constance. She presented it to St Marys when she opened the Hamilton Memorial Hall. The mallet he gave to his then 14 year old son Herbert

'that little pickle'.

Its whereabouts are not known. He probably wore it out!

The Foundation Stone.

TO THE GLORY OF GOD
AND IN LOVING MEMORY OF
MAUD HAMILTON
THIS CHURCH IS ERECTED BY
HER HUSBAND
THE FIRST VICAR OF CHRIST CHURCH WOKING
AND PREVIOUSLY VICAR OF ST JOHNS
WHO LAID THIS FOUNDATION STONE
OCTOBER 15TH 1906
ON THE 25TH ANNIVERSARY
OF THEIR WEDDING

The silver plated trowel used for laying the foundation stone. The small plaque is a replica of the foundation stone.

The inscription on the trowel reads

*'Presented to the Rev WFT Hamilton, on the occasion of the laying of the foundation stone of the church of St Mary of Bethany in the parish of Christ Church, Woking, on the 15th October, 1906
E R Price Deveraux Vicar*

'A' Alpha   'Ω' Omega

'Mary hath chosen'

'that good part'

The East Window.

'Mary Knelt at His Feet'

'Mary Fell at His Feet'

'Mary Anointed His Feet'

'ihs'

The *ihs* monogram is an abbreviation or shortening of Jesus' name in Greek to the first three letters. Thus ΙΗΣΟΥΣ, ιησυς (*iēsus*, "Jesus"), is shortened to ΙΗΣ (iota-eta-sigma), sometimes transliterated into Latin or English characters as IHS or IHC.

The east window depicts 3 scenes from the Bible.

The left hand panel. ***Mary knelt at His feet*** is taken from Luke ch10 v39. Mary sits at Jesus' feet listening to him while Martha, Mary's sister, is busy preparing a meal in the background.

The centre panel. ***Mary annointed His feet*** is taken from John ch12 v3. Mary, Martha and Lazarus, their brother, give a dinner in Jesus' honour. Again Martha prepares the food while Mary annoints Jesus' feet with approx 1/2 a litre of an expensive perfume called nard.

The right hand panel. ***Mary fell at His feet*** is taken from John ch11 v32. Lazarus had died four days earlier and when Jesus arrived Mary ran to him and fell at his feet.

At the top of the window are the words ***Mary hath chosen**** and ****that good part*** taken from Luke ch10 v42. Jesus suggests to Martha that Mary is doing the right thing by listening to Him.

The window was manufactured by Heaton, Butler & Bayne of 14 Garrick Street Covent Garden London. They were one of the largest and most successful stained glass designers and manufacturers of the 1900s and known world wide until they closed in 1953.

Clement Heaton a glass painter and James Butler a lead glazier began making stained glass in 1855 sharing premises with Clayton and Bell, a new firm of glass designers with whom they shared their technical expertise. In 1862 Robert Bayne, a pre Raphaelite artist, became chief designer. Heaton, Butler & Bayne exhibited at the 1867 Paris Exhibition. Their work includes Westminster Abbey and Peterborough Cathedral. The very bright colours of their earlier work had by the turn of the century been replaced by muted colours and more lifelike figures as in this window.

The subject, Mary, was chosen by William Hamilton; Caröe designed the whole window and Robert Bayne designed the glass.

Heaton, Butler & Bayne also manufactured the east windows for Christ Church Woking and St Pauls Maybury. When William Hamilton was vicar of Christ Church the plain leaded glass in the east window was replaced in 1897 with a five light window in memory of his sister-in-law.

The reredos was designed by W D Caröe, and carved by Nathaniel Hitch of London. Nathaniel Hitch (1846-1938) was a very well known sculptor who worked for a number of famous architects. Examples of his work can be found in Westminster Abbey, Truro Cathedral and Cardiff Castle.

The relief features a family of four, not the Hamiltons, with Jesus in the centre. William Hamilton's family never lived at home together as a family of four but he knew they would be united in Heaven. Jesus appears in glory, with angels either side on the brackets. The inscription below is taken from 2 Thessalonians ch 2 v 1 and reads

'Our gathering together unto Him'

The report of the consecration in the Woking News and Mail 8th November 1907 said

'There is a rich coloured reredos...'.

The wood as shown here was originally painted dark green with gold lining and highlights. In 1956 with the guidance of

The Reredos.

the diocesan architect the green paint was overpainted in a grained beech finish. It was probably thought to look 'high church' and out of keeping with the plainer more modern style of the building. The figures have always have been white.

At the same time the curtains were removed from either side. They were going to be replaced but the overall opinion was that the sanctuary looked much lighter without them.

The wording on the reredos was the subject of William

Hamilton's sermon on 10th November 1907 the first Sunday after the consecration of St Mary's. The sermon was repeated on 11th November 1962, on the occasion of the 50th anniversary of the consecration, by Rev Raymond Lee.

Detail of main relief of Reredos.

The photograph shows a clay mock-up of the angels which appear on brackets either side of the main relief. The instruments were changed from a psaltery and harp in the photograph to trumpets in the final sculpture. This is taken from an album of photographs collected by W D Carôe.

Photograph of angels.

THE EAST WINDOW AND REREDOS
AS WELL AS THE CHURCH
WERE ERECTED IN LOVING MEMORY OF

MAUD HAMILTON

BY HER HUSBAND

HER SWEET AND HOLY CHARACTER
SUGGESTED THE CHURCH'S NAME
"ST MARY OF BETHANY"
AND THE SUBJECTS OF THE WINDOW

MARY SAT AT HIS FEET

ST LUKE X 39

MARY ANNOINTED HIS FEET

ST JOHN XII 3

MARY FELL AT HIS FEET

ST JOHN XI 32

"MARY HATH CHOSEN THAT GOOD PART
WHICH SHALL NOT BE TAKEN AWAY FROM HER"

WE LOOK FOR THE
COMING OF OUR LORD AND
OUR GATHERING TOGETHER UNTO HIM

2 THESS II 1

The Memorial Plaque.

The alabaster memorial plaque is situated on the south wall of the chancel and commemorates the dedication of St Mary of Bethany church. It carries descriptions of the stained glass window and the inscription on the Reredos.

The font is almost certainly a Caröe design and may have been made by Nathaniel Hitch. It is octagonal is plan sitting on a rectangular plinth with a matching stone step. There is an oak cover bearing around the edge the inscription

'REPENT AND BE BAPTISED'

The font was originally situated at the 'back', west end, of the church exactly in the centre of the current main entrance. Baptisms were usually held in the afternoons when the baptism party would sit in the baptistry. See drawing on page 27 for the layout of the proposed baptistry. When baptisms during morning services became usual the congregation would have to turn round to face the back of the church. The positioning of the font near the main door is traditional and signifies welcoming.

It was moved to it's present location in March 1956 when the west porch was added.

The table, communion rails, prayer desk, choir stalls and pulpit were manufactured by E Bowman & Sons Ltd of Stamford Lincolnshire to W D Caröe designs.   The last two being in store now. The column casings are not mentioned in Bowman's records so may have been made by E C Hughes carpenters.

The Font.

The bell was cast by Mears and Stainbank of 34 Whitechapel Road London E. It weighs 224lb and is hung in a bell-cote on the west elevation. The bell cost £22 10s 0d (£22.50p) when new plus £2 10s od (£2.50p) for delivery and fitting. Today this is a standard bell which is kept in stock. The price - £2904 plus packing and carriage.

Mears and Stainbank now trades as The Whitechapel Bell Foundry. It is recognised as the oldest businesses in the UK with an unbroken line back to Robert Chamberlain in 1420.

During some building work in 1992 an inspection of the bell cote showed up cracks in the brickwork and the bell. For safety the bell was not rung again and was taken down. Closer inspection of the bell showed 2 vertical cracks starting from the bolt hole in the top. One of which had turned horizontally and worked its way around a quarter of the circumference. The PCC decided the bell was not a priority for funds, but allowed an independent restoration fund to accept voluntary donations.

The bell ready for transporting to the repairers in 1999

A suggestion to join with churches all over the country to ring in the New Year at noon on January 1st 2000 was a spur to renew efforts to proceed quickly with restoration and raise the necessary outstanding money.

The bell was taken to Sound Weld a specialist bell repairer in Cambridge where the cracks were opened out and rewelded. After repair it was transported to Nicholson Engineering in Lyme Regis, Dorset, a specialist bellhanger, for refurbishment and assembly of the headstock, bearings, clapper etc.

After repairs and repointing of the turret the bell was rehung in June 1999 in time to ring in the new millenium.

An Undated Postcard, probably photographed very soon after completion of the church. The **organ** may have been installed which would make the date after 1914. An harmonium was used until the installation of the organ. Interesting points to note are the **electric lights** which were innovative enough to get a mention in the Woking News and Mail report of the dedication. The same lights were also installed in the chancel; note the shades and how low all the lights are hung. The deep **south windows** before the Hamilton Hall was built. The internal **porch** to the north door, which was removed when the church centre was built. The **reredos** which was painted in rich colours. The

An early postcard of St Mary of Bethany Interior.

curtains either side of the reredos. Two rows of **choir stalls either side of the chancel** for boys and men only. 2 extra rows of stalls were added for women in 1926. Chairs in front of the lectern facing across the church. Could these have been for the women of the choir, or perhaps the boys? The **chairs** with the original kneelers and note the reserved seat for the deputy Church Warden where the 'pole' is positioned. There was only one deputy warden until the new parish was formed. You did not dare to sit there! Initially the seating in the centre aisle was **rented** and the remaining seats were free. The **pulpit** is now in storage with the choir stalls. During redecoration of the church interior in November 1965 the ceiling between the rafters in the **chancel** was painted white to lighten the appearance as was the brick arch above the east window.

The organ was manufactured by Alfred Hunter and Son in 1913 who were trading at the time (1907-1929) from 87 High Street Clapham, London. Alfred Hunter the founder died in 1911 aged 84.

In 1935 the manual bellows were replaced with Hunter's 'Discus' Electrical Blowing Equipment. Alfred Hunter and Sons were taken over in 1937 by Henry Willis and Sons 34 Marlborough Grove, Old Kent Rd, London . Henry Willis still produce pipe organs today in Petersfield, Hampshire.

The Organ.
The pipes are
dummies; the
works
are behind.

The organ was initially maintained by Hunter followed by Willis then others. Rushworth & Draeper have been servicing and repairing the organ since 1962. There has been subsequent cleaning, releathering; and a Fifteenth 2' stop was installed in place of the Great Open Diapason in 1976.

In the summer of 1980 during the singing of a psalm a bottom note stuck open and the organ was switched off. A five week long full clean and overhaul with further timely releathering costing £6000 was carried out by Rushworth and Dreaper which involved removing all 1200 pipes. The organ was back in service for harvest. A photograph appeared in the Woking News & Mail showing Norman Norgate, the vicar, and Cyril Pawley, the choirmaster and organist, holding one of the largest pipes. St Marys held a caption competition for the photograph and the winner was

Henry Doughty
c 1950.

'*...and at 50,000ft it explodes*
and deluges the Kremlin with
copies of St Mary's newsletter'

A parishioner donated an Alexander harmonium to celebrate the dedication of the church. This was used until 1914 when the organ was installed. The harmonium was then moved to the Kingsway Hall. It may have been replaced in 1958 after extensive repairs were diagnosed and a request was put out for a replacement. Unfortunately whichever one it was it met its demise in the fire which destroyed the hall.

The organ was registered in 1949 with
the National Pipe Organ Register of Cambridge
Ref N13975

Organ Specification

Couplers

Swell to Pedal   Swell to Great   Swell octave
Swell suboctave   Great to Pedal

	Compass low	Compass high	Notes	Enclosed
Pedal	C	f1	30	N
Great	C	c4	61	N
Swell	C	c4	61	Y

Department	Stop name	Pitch
Pedal	1 Open Diapason	16
	2 Bourdon	16
	3 Flute Bass	8

Department	Stop name	Pitch
Great	4 Dulciana	8
	5 Large Open Diapason	8
	6 Hohl Flute	8
	7 Small Open Diapason	8
	8 Claribel Flute	4
	9 Octave	4

Department	Stop name	Pitch
Swell	10 Geigen Diapason	8
	11 Rohr Flute	8
	12 Viol d'Orchestre	8
	13 Voix Celeste	8
	14 Principal	4
	15 Horn	8
	16 Tremulant	

1, 3, 3 composition pedals   3 thumb pistons to each manual

THIS ORGAN
WAS DEDICATED
TO THE GLORY OF GOD
9TH FEBRUARY 1914
E R PRICE DEVEREUX

*The plaque
on the organ.
E R Price
Devereux
was the vicar
of the parish.*

To celebrate the fiftieth anniversary of the dedication
of the organ Barry Rose, Guildford Cathedral's organist, was
invited to play after the evening service on 24th May 1964.

The Original South Elevation Entrance 1907

A portion of a 1907 postcard which shows the main entrance; the small door.

This photo, right, shows the original 'temporary' entrance in the 'temporary' south wall. The wall would have been demolished had the south aisle been built. This is the small door in the photo. The door nearest is the vestry door.

This doorway still exists, below, and is now used as the connecting door between the church and the hall.

The original door, now used to access the hall. The alcove was to be the main entrance.

West Porch and New Entrance 1956

When St Marys was designed the Architect W D Caröe had included a baptistry and entrance on the west elevation. William Hamilton had not included this cost in his gift. The new main entrance and porch were added in 1956 at a cost of £660 to give a focal point to the York Road elevation. The porch was dedicated on Sunday evening 19th February 1956 by Dr H C Montgomery Campbell, Bishop of London, formerly Bishop of Guildford (1949-1956). This was his last official engagement before retirement.

A photo from a magazine cover showing the newly completed porch and new entrance c1956.

Gifts of furnishings were made by various members including; a table and curtains to keep out the draughts. A bench was presented by Nancy Richardson, Daphne Evans mother, in memory of her husband.

The porch was demolished in 1974 with the commencement of building work on the Church Centre.

Architect: David Evelyn Nye and Partners   1960
Builder: A W Middleton and Co
Cost: £7100

The idea for a hall on the church site had been in mind since Rev Jack Marshall's time as vicar around 1946. An anonymous donation of £100 was made to form the nucleus of the Hamilton Memorial Hall Fund whose secretary was Mr Francis Walmsley. There was little money around after the war but the idea was at the forefront of projects. In 1953 Jack Marshall remarked that *'40 small children in the vicarage dining room on a Sunday morning is a major operation!'* 1953, Coronation year, unfortunately had it's own expenditure in the form of retiling the church roof. So the hall was put on hold again. The fund was 'live' as part of the Bishops Appeal started in 1944. By September 1957 it stood at £450 when the PCC unanimously agreed that the need for a hall was becoming increasingly urgent in view of the growing work and activities. The Kingsway Hall was in use every night of the week by then. The Building Committee consisted of Lt Col GGS Clarke, who had known William Hamilton personally, PG Warren and H Yates.

The Hamilton Memorial Hall was built onto the south side of the church at a cost of £7500 on what had always been a lawn. This area was intended from the original plans to be used for extending the nave of the church with a south aisle to mirror the north aisle. If you look above the vestry door you will notice that the gable end wall was only half built and the brickwork was left unfinished until the kitchen refurbishment when the brick toothing was infilled. The same can be seen in this photograph where the butresses have the mortar joints raked out ready to take the proposed baptistry. The hall was officially opened by Constance Hamilton and dedicated by the RR Ivor Watkins DD, Bishop of Guildford on Saturday 8th October 1960.

The Hamilton Memorial Hall. This photo was taken as work was starting on the Church Centre building.

Included in the hall were a kitchen, toilets, a stage, a connecting door to the old vestry lobby and a connecting door into the church, using the same opening that had been the original entrance in the south wall. The main entrance to the hall was through a pair of doors in the west elevation. These opened onto a corridor which encircled the stage.

A plan of the Hall.

Kitchen

Toilets

Stage

The Hamilton Memorial Hall looking towards the stage.

*Looking
towards the
kitchen end of
the hall 2005.*

*The Stage
looking from
the kitchen end
of the hall
featuring a
YCF band
from the 1960's.*

Architect: Donald, Hamilton & Montefiore   **1974**
Builder: James Longley & Co Ltd
Cost: £57,000

With the demise of the Kingsway Hall a lot of pressure was put on the space available for church activities and affiliated groups. The Hamilton Hall, choir vestry and Vicar's vestry being the only spaces available on church premises.

Among those made 'homeless' by the loss of the Kingsway Hall were Pathfinders, Youth Fellowship, Cubs, Scouts, Brownies and Guides.

They all had to be accommodated in the Hamilton Hall. On Sundays Climbers and Explorers used the hall, vestry *and* kitchen. Yes, the kitchen was used as a classroom. The vicarage and neighbouring members houses were also called into use.

A crèche was held nearby for the 10am family service. The then current vicar Norman Norgate said:-

> '... the plan is to encircle the worship area; Christ and all his people at the centre and all the facilities we need around us....a family centre radiant with the love the Spirit of Jesus pours into our hearts, overflowing to the neighbourhood of Mount Hermon and Kingsway'.

The affected church groups had by this time laid claim to the space they required, Climbers leader Jean Harrison was very excited about the prospect of having 3 year olds in a teaching room adjacent to the toilets. Joan Methold, Pathfinder leader, said that the current facilities only allowed room for half of the 40 regulars, Richard Cowan, Youth Fellowship leader, bemoaned the loss of the back room of the Kingsway Hall as it had been the YF base. A new one was vitally important as young people value a base/headquarters very highly. The Explorers used the choir vestry and leader Mary Certin said that you could never be sure when the choir might reappear at the end of a service. A new room would enable lessons to be prepared in advance of the start of a service. The A3 size newsletter dated 13th January 1974 reproduced here aimed to inform and call upon members to donate £15,000 towards the £57,000 estimated cost. £42,000 was already available. Donald, Hamilton and Montefiore were appointed as architects with Derek Montifiore being our architect. He had lived in Woking

and was instrumental in setting up the Second Achilles Housing Association: Woodham Place and Achilles Place where a number of St Mary's members have been residents.

Some of those involved in the project included Rupert Pilkington-Chairman of the Church Centre Planning Group, David Hughes, John Bednall, Peter Hancock and Ray Marks. The contractor was James Longley & Co Ltd.

The Church Centre was officially opened with a service of thanksgiving and dedication held at 2.30pm on Sunday 1st December 1974 attended by the Mayor and Mayoress of Woking and the Bishop of Guildford.

The external design of the church centre would probably be termed 'unsympathetic' today, but was of the current modern style when built. With hindsight access to the various rooms should have been given more consideration. A corridor would have given easier access without the necessity of passing through one room for access to another.

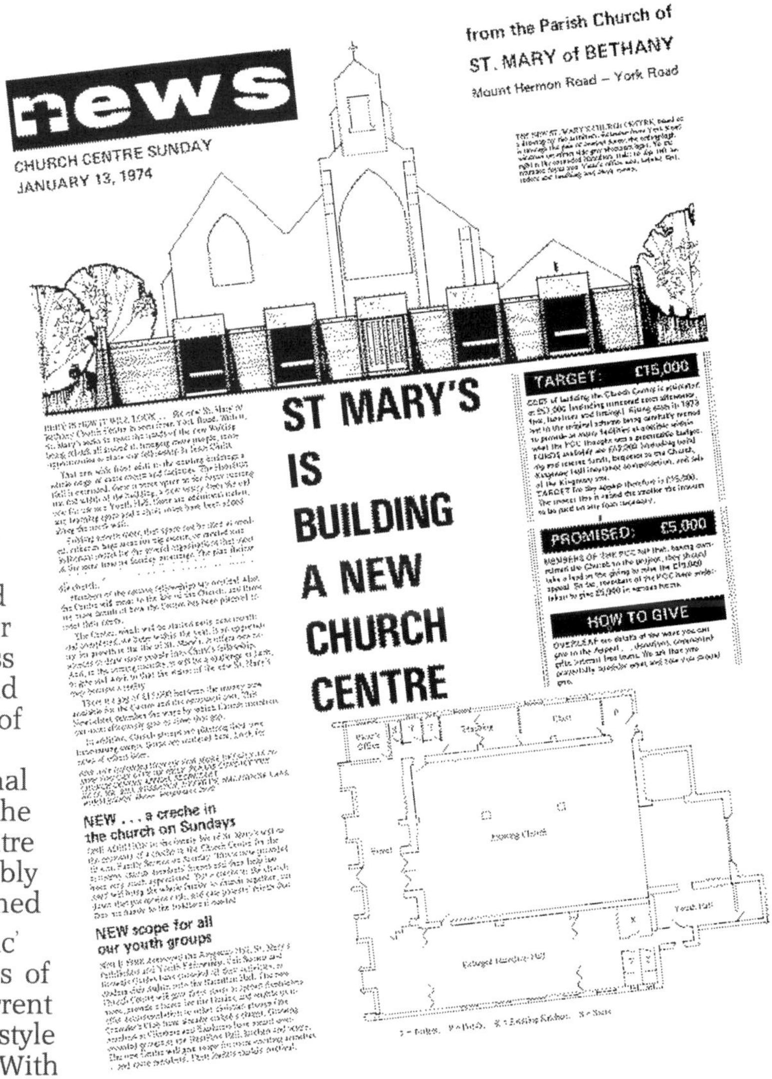

New Church Centre Newsletter.

Refurbishment of Church Worship Area 1994

Architect: Mr Ivor Plummer RIBA
Contractor: Wickens of Chertsey
Manager: Mr M Bolton
Cost: £75,000

In recent years the greatest change to the church building has come with the internal refurbishment. This inevitably caused friction amongst Church members as it involved changing the orientation of the seating so that the focus was on the south wall instead of looking east towards the chancel. The reason for the change was to bring all the congregation closer to the centre - a modern layout for a church.

The Grade II listing does not prevent alterations to the furnishings. The internal layout with the seating facing the chancel. was both original and traditional. A faculty had to be obtained from the diocese for permission to carry out changes. All changes were made without being permanent or causing damage to the original layout so that at a future date, if required, the original layout can be reinstated.

The back cloth. See overleaf for description.

The choir stalls and pulpit were removed and stored in the roof space above the Hamilton Hall. The original chairs were sold. A raised dais was installed on the south wall. The 2nd World War memorial rails and radiators were relocated. The floor was carpeted with tiles and new upholstered chairs purchased. The heating system was upgraded with additional convector heaters, three ceiling fans and a new electronic programmer.

Experiments were carried out to find the best layout for dais and seating. Due to the temporary nature of the trial period the church was obligated to return the seating to it's original layout if required. This was done a number of times, especially for weddings, when requested.

Two overhead projectors were purchased to enable songs and hymns to be shown on the wall either side of the backdrop. Two reasons are cited for this arrangement. 1) Heads could now be raised rather than stuck into books. 2) With new songs coming along with greater frequency it reduced the cost of continually buying new song books.

The projectors have also proved extremely useful for many other aspects of worship including the display of sermon notes and notices. Today the

Looking towards entrance doors in west elevation.

church worship area is used for many purposes with the seating being so flexible. Within half an hour all the seating can be rearranged and tables assembled for, say, a supper for 120 people and then put back for worship in another half

Chairs and tables set out for a lunch.

an hour. The area now looks good, is larger, has better heating, and has better acoustics than the hall.

A back cloth was designed and made by Juliet Hemingray and hung on a 3 arched panels which covers the centre of the three south windows. Juliet previously designed and made the robes for Dr Carey's enthronement as Archbishop of Canterbury. The back cloth design caused a great deal of discussion and this, edited, sheet was published to clarify the design.

An Interpretation?

... we should avoid thinking in terms of "the interpretation" and we must also avoid treating the backcloth as "a work of art" with clever symbolism of religious ideas. It should instead be seen as a potential tool for the Lord's use to speak to us individually or to heighten our awareness of different facets of His character as we worship Him each Sunday.

Design Concepts
...certain basic concepts have been built into the design by Juliet Hemingray which may be of value if the Lord wishes to teach us something new of Himself through the design. These ideas and associations are as follows:
     - THE CROSS is the dominant feature of the design - the only means by which we can be "put right" with God to restore the -close relationship which He had originally intended Man should have with Him.
     - to the right of the cross are the "silver" THORNS which together with the cross are symbols of the suffering and humiliation endured by Jesus for us.
     - the RED colours are associated with the release of the power of the Holy Spirit at Pentecost while the BLUE speaks of the heavens, space, eternity and those things which lie beyond the grasp of our finite minds....

Extended Kitchen 2000

Architect: Trevor J Tilley Dip Arch RIBA
Contractor: Mr M Charman
Manager: Mr J Brooks
Cost: £55,000

The original kitchen was built with the Hamilton Hall in 1961 and had been refurbished a couple of times, mainly with paint!. In the 1990's it was becoming increasingly noticeable that it could not cope with the number of functions for which catering was required, nor did it meet ever changing legislation for hygiene and safety.

Events such as Men's Suppers, Cameo, Alpha Courses, Bethany Babes and Concerts all require different types of catering and so a new kitchen was planned. Some argument arose about whether this should wait until a more comprehensive plan could be implemented, to improve access to the various rooms and halls. The main failing of the Church Centre being that access to some rooms could not be gained without walking through one room or the church to gain access into another. However the need to service the growing number of evangelistic groups and meetings was deemed to be of greater importance. The new larger kitchen features the latest in stainless steel and other hygienic apparatus and includes hygienic paint! A lot of the finishing work, including decorating, was done by church members. The refurbishment work also included the building of a run of storage cupboards across the hall and upgrading the toilet and baby changing facilities.

The new larger kitchen.

Heating

Below the original vestry is a boiler house. The heating system was installed during the building of the church. William Hamilton was very keen on warmth! He had similar systems installed in the church in Cromer and previously in Christ Church. The original boiler was coke fired which meant lighting it and refuelling it at precise times to meet service requirements. The church employed a stoker to carry out this task. He must have been an early riser. Later the system was upgraded to include an oil burning boiler and more recently changed to a gas fired boiler. During the worship area refurbishment a new sophisticated control system was installed along with three fans in the roof. For the first time in 100 years the church was now warm and welcoming for *any* service or activity at *any* time on any day of the week.

Lighting

The Woking News and Mail report of the dedication of St Mary of Bethany Church mentioned that electric lighting had been installed. Electricity was in it's very early days and still of interest. Woking was a very early user of electricity and a latecomer to gas. Street lighting was put out to tender and electricity beat gas. Electric street lighting was installed in 1895. However the electricity supply proved to be unreliable and so all the street lighting was converted to gas in 1902 - when most cities and large towns were converting theirs to electricity - and it remained gas until 1931. The street lamp at the mount Hermon Road entrance is original other than the lamp unit and of course the post box is the original Victorian one.

The Garden

When the church was designed a south aisle was proposed for the future. The site for this, on the south side of the church was laid to lawn and disappeared under the Hamilton Memorial Hall when it was built. The east end had a semi circular lawn under the window with gates at either end of the plot and footpaths leading round. The central opening was created for cars when the garden was turned into a car park. In 1956 a footpath was laid around the north elevation where a bicycle shed was situated.

1953
Roof retiled. This work had been noted as requiring attention during the war years.

1954
Church Improvement Fund
Resurface paths. Lay new path to north elevation.
Red carpet for sanctuary generously donated.

2002
Vicar's Vestry A major refurbishment of the old vestry was undertaken. This room had become a storage area for Bethany Babe's toys, kitchen requisites, replacement light bulbs etc. With the new kitchen and storage cupboards now in use it was decided to create a bright modern office for the use of vicar and other clergy.

The huge new gas meter that was installed during the reordering was moved to the boiler room and complete redecoration included repairs, rewiring, a heater, telephone points, a ceiling fan and rehanging the door.

2004
A computer, projector and screen were installed to allow the projection of words of songs and hymns, notices, liturgy, and multi media presentations to be easily viewed.

2005
New lighting installed in Chancel. This almost returned the lighting to the original layout. although the glass shades could not be matched exactly.

2006
Extensive refurbishment of 27 Hawthorn Road.

A reproduction from the Woking News and Mail
Is there a spelling mistake in the first line?

WOKING NEWS AND MAIL
Friday 8th November 1907

WOKING'S NEW CHURCH.

REV. W. F. T. HAMILTONS GIFT.

Dedicated by the Bishop of

Winchester.

On Monday afternoon, in the pressence of a very large congregation, the new church of St Mary of Bethany, in Mount Hermon Road Woking, was dedicated, by the Bishop of Winchester. Some time before leaving Woking, the Rev. W. F. T. Hamilton, Vicar of Cromer, formerly Vicar of Christ Church secured a site for the church between the Mount Hermon and York Roads. This together with the church, he has presented to his parish in memory of his late wife. Mr. Hamilton laid the foundation stone in October last year, on the twenty-fifth anniversary of his wedding day. The contract for the erection of the building was placed in the hands of Mr. Hughes, of Wokingham, and the architect was Mr W. D. Caroe F.S.A., of Westminster. Mr.Hughes has also carried out the heating installation. The building is of red brick with stone sparsely used in the window traceries. In the arches and string courses red tiles have been freely used, imparting a novel and dignified effect. When completed the church will consist of a nave, north and south aisles without, clerestories, a deep chancel, an organ chamber, on the north side, and vestry on the other. The south aisle and eastern porch have not yet been erected. There is a rich coloured reredos from the architect's design, illustrative of the words 'Our gathering together unto Thee,' which are inscribed on it. This is surmounted by an east window, depicting scenes from the history of St. Mary of Bethany. The sculpture and the reredos was executed by Mr.Hitch, of London. The fittings of the church-choir stalls, pulpit, columns, etc.- are all bass wood. There is accommodation for a congregation of 500 persons, but when completed, by the addition of the south aisle this will be increased to 700. The interior is well ventilated, and lighted by electricity, and, with its open timber roofs and carved wood fittings, presents a spacious appearance.

It is understood that the edifice will, in a few years time, become the parish church of a new ecclesiastical district, but. for the present it will be under the vicar of Christ Church. Mr. H. C. Rowntree has undertaken the duties of organist and choirmaster, and Mr. E. Collins is churchwarden. For the present Mr. J. A. Ness is acting as his deputy. Mr.G. Beale has been appointed verger and clerk. Mr. and Mrs. C. F. Kenord, of Northaw Lodge, have presented a solid silver communion service to the church, in memory of their only son, who died recently. The panels of the Holy Table were worked by Miss Agnes Stanley. (sister of the late Mrs. Hamilton), and the communion cloth by Miss C. Hamilton.

As in the other churches in the parish, half the seats are to be rented, and half free. A good harmonium has been procured, and this together with cassocks, surplices, books, safe, vestry furniture, etc., will be provided by the members of the congregation. Towards this the Rev. F. D. Morice has given £5. Mrs Hodgson £1 1s., a friend (per Mrs.Hodgson) £2, and Miss Gouldsmith (for books) £3.

THE CONSECRATION

There was a large gathering at the ceremony on Tuesday. The Bishop of Winchester was accompanied by the Rev. J. R. Spittal as chaplain, and the other clergy present were the Rev. W. F. T. Hamilton, the Rev. E. R. Price Devereux (Vicar of Christ Church) the Rev. A. R. Marriott, the Rev. H. R. Bates and. the Rev. H. J. Mowll (curates), the Rev. Canon Skelton, R.D., the Rev. F. J. Oliphant (Vicar of Woking), the Rev. J. M. Harris and the Rev. A. Phelps (St. John's), the Rev. Norman Pares and the Rev. J. H. C. Evelegh (Horsell), the Rev. H. S. Acworth (Chobham), the Rev. H. E. Smith (Horsell), the Rev. J. Osborne and the Rev.

E. Skuse (Pyrford)., the Rev. H. V. Elliott (Send), the.Rey. W. H. Gay (Gordon Boys' Home), the Rev. E.W. Field (chaplain at St. Peter's. Home), the Rev. W. E. Peters (St. Saviour's, Guildford), the Rev. F. J. Lawrie, the Rev. Wootton Fitz-Paine (Dorset), the Rev. W. A. Challacombe (Vicar of New Malden), the Rev. D. Macdonald (Mitcham), and Bishop Evington (Japan).

The Bishop was received at the west entrance by the clergy :and churchwardens, and as the procession was made to the chancel, Psalm 122 was sung by the choir and congregation. The dedicatory prayers were said by the Bishop and after the hymn, 'We love the place of God.' a shortened form of evening prayer was intoned by the Rev. E. R. Price Devereux, assisted by the Rev. H. J. Mowll. Psalm 84 was sung, and the special lessons read by Canon Skelton and the Rev. F.J. Oliphant.

THE BISHOP'S ADDRESS.

After the hymn, 'All people that on earth do dwell,' the Bishop gave an address, taking as his text, St. John xi. 2, 'It was that Mary which anointed the Lord with ointment, and wiped his feet with her hair.' They had met, said his Lordship, that afternoon for the solemn service of the dedication of that church-the fulfilment of many prayers and intercessions for the, extensions of Church life in the town end the neighbourhood for the advancement of the glory of God, for the deepening of spiritual life. Thankfully they dedicated to the glory of God, and to the memory of one whom He had taken to Himself that spacious and dignified church which was going to be the centre of the spiritual life in that neighbourhood. How solemn, and sacred were the thoughts that surged through the mind as they thought of the generation upon generation who would there pour their blessings out to God, and the thought he would give to them was the thought bound up with the name which that Church, would bear -the name of St. Mary of Bethany. He could not help associating the act of dedication with the act of St. Mary of Bethany, who on that day, so shortly before the Lord's passion and death, poured upon Him the precious ointment-a dedication of her wealth, gifts and affection, in token of strong personal love. There was the secret of every pure act of devotion: that personal devotion was the one spring and source ofevery genuine dedication, and that Church was dedicated in the name of St. Mary of Bethany; herself the example of loving and generous dedication to her divine Lord. She was one of a little household in a little village near Jerusalem, but her name was held in honour whenever the Gospel message was preached. A new church called by the name of Mary of Bethany was a reminder of the Church's work   that it was a work of love, and a witness against a spirit of worldliness. Like Mary of Bethany the Church continually made her sacrifices of love and devotion. The work of offering was going on still: it had never ceased. Ever since that time the Church had been offering up her great offering of personal affection and love in the dedication of any sort of gift to the glory of God and the honour of the Redeemer. No gift that was made to the church was really acceptable in the Lord's sight which did not come from the same feeling that prompted St. Mary of Bethany to make her offering.

A FRESH CENTRE OF WORSHIP.

Continuing, the Bishop said, 'I speak of the unbelieving attitude, cold and unsympathetic, which looks on with something approaching disapproval. It says, What is the good of the expenditure of all this money? Could it not rather have been expended on the poor? Could it not have been distributed with greater effect. The ancient and modern endowments of the Church of England are wholly inadequate for the purpose for which they were originally given by good and de- voted men and women. Ancient and modern endowments produced   five   millions   a   year- all adequate to the needs. In addition, about seven millions are voluntarily contr- buted by Churchpeople for the work , and besides, that another sum of £850,000 is being devoted to the cause of foreign missions by the Church. The world, no doubt, will look on and say, "Why is this waste?" The

Church, we pray God, will go on increasing more and more of its devotion and dedication to the Lord Jesus Christ, being persuaded that it can give to no better object than that for the honour of our Saviour. I pray God that this Church, which we dedicate in the name of St. Mary of Bethany, will always help to promote the knowledge and love of God, will spread the Gospel of the Lord Jesus Christ, and will make a fresh centre in this place for the preaching of His Word and for building up in this town and neighbourhood the personal devotion to the Lord Jesus Christ: that is the one rock and foundation upon which the Church is built. Christ is the only remedy of the world's ills. We are not ashamed to put Him ever first and foremost, and where He is known and where He is loved, there will come that which is needed for the good of the country. There will come love, peace and long suffering goodness, purity and truth, and the blessings of a Christian life. Here in this new church, which we dedicate to his glory - a very beautiful and stately building, likely to last for centuries- here we dedicate it specially to the one who loved her Lord like Mary of Bethany. Here may an unfailing offering be made by the Church of Christ, and may the spirit of Christ Himself reign and rule in the hearts and in the consciences of. those who come here, and may the love of Christ give comfort to all who worship here, for this life and the one to come.'

NOTES AND COMMENTS

Two important and interesting events in connection with parochial life are recorded this week. One is the opening of the Parish Hall, a commodious and extremely convenient building, at Horsell, and the other the consecration of the new church at Mount Hermon, the handsome gift of the Rev. W. F. T. Hamilton, to his old parish, in loving memory of his wife. At Horsell the new hall will form a much-needed centre for parochial work of many kinds. The absence of such a place has been long felt, but it is only through the persistent efforts of the Vicar (the Rev. Norman Pares), and a few enthusiastic helpers, that the scheme has been carried to a successful conclusion. As to the church at Mount Hermon, its Consecration marks an epoch in the history of the parish, for eventually it is, to become the centre of a new ecclesiastical district. For the present it remains a new and important addition to the church accommodation of the populous parish of Christ Church, and it will always stand as a monument, not only to the memory of her to, whom it is erected as a memorial, but also to love and affection which the Rev. W. F. T, Hamilton has for the parish in which he laboured so long and so zealously.

SCRIBO SECUNDUS.

Notes and Comments
was part of the
"Editorial"
in the same issue

Also in the same issue:-

On Saturday (2nd) afternoon
the Bishop of Dorking
dedicated the new Horsell
Parish Hall.

The first service at St Mary of Bethany, after the dedication, was the 8.00 am Communion service on Sunday November 10th November 1907 taken by the vicar Rev E R Price-Devereux. The number of communicants was 38. This was about average for all services for at least 15 years. The first recorded congregation over 100 (105) was Easter Day 1910, These numbers are for communicants at Communion services. There was no requirement to record numbers for other services. The offertory of £1 2s 9d (£1 14p) went to the poor fund.

William Hamilton lead the 11.00am service, his theme being 2 Thessolonians ch 2 v 1, '...our gathering together unto him'. The offertory of £8 3s 5¼d (£8 17p) went to support 'Our Own Missionary'. This may have been Charlotte Bacon.

There were two more services that day. At 3.00pm Herbert Mowll, the curate who was chosen to run St Mary of Bethany as a chapel-of-ease spoke to an unknown number of worshippers about Mary of Bethany and at 6.30pm The vicar again spoke on Psalm 63 v2 'I have seen God in the sanctuary'.

St Mary of Bethany became a parish in its own right on 28th November 1923. The parish was originally to be formed within a few years of the church being built but the population did not increase at the rate initially envisaged. There are a number of reasons for the slow growth. The houses to the south of the town were larger, and therefore had fewer residents and secondly the First World War depressed land and house sales. Remember that all the land in and around Woking was either heathland, farmland or nursery land and all new housing was going up on what today we call greenfield sites. There was a financial incentive to have a parish of 4000 inhabitants because it attracted an endowment of £200 per year from the Ecclesiastical Commissioners. In 1910 the parish population was calculated as 3700 and it took another 13 years for the population to increase by only 300 to the 4000 required.

The parish boundary was drawn up at the time of St Mary of Bethany church being built. The map reproduced here from the first parish magazine of June 1924 is quite a bit older than 1924, probably from around the turn of the century, as it shows no houses along the western end of York Road or Mount Hermon Road. If you remember the Kingsway Hall you will see that it is shown in the wrong position on the map: it should be approximately by the S of Kingsway.

PLAN OF ST MARY'S PARISH.

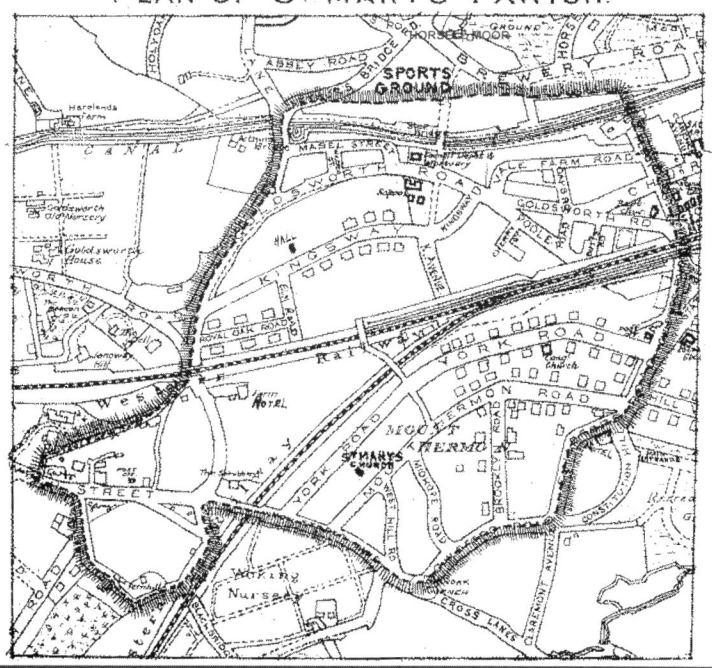

The first Parish Boundary 1924.

The parish map did not change until the 3rd April 1959 when a wholesale realignment of parish boundaries in and around Woking was undertaken. The post war boom of house building had created a number of large new local authority estates including Maybury, Byfleet, Elmbridge, and Barnsbury, and of course the London County Council estate on Sheerwater. Proposals for the realignment of the parish boundaries came about because St Pauls was to be divided from Christ Church to become a separate parish. Gen C H Geake Hon Secretary of the Guildford Pastoral Committee proposed that the boundary changes be based on two principals: -

1) ...a more equitable distribution of the increased population of Woking.

2) ...to bring the majority of parishioners within a reasonable distance of their parish church.

This was determined as 15 minutes walking time and that it should not be necessary to own a motor car in order to take part in regular worship. There was much discussion about walking distances; the underlying motive being the possible loss of more prosperous areas to another parish. St Mary of Bethany would lose one small area, Horsell Moor, north of the Basingstoke Canal to St Mary's Horsell, and a larger area bounded by the canal to the north, the railway to the south,

Step Bridge to the west and Percy Street (Victoria Way) to the east to Christ Church. At the same time all the houses in Claremont Avenue, Poplar Grove, Salisbury Road, Wych Hill Way, Turnoak Lane, Blackness Lane, Old Hill and Hillside were transferred to St Marys together with further parts of Blackbridge Road, Guildford Road and Wych Hill Lane, most of Constitution Hill, parts of Egley Road, all the new houses in Turnoak Avenue and the majority of Woking Park, including the Swimming Pool. The new Barnsbury estate was also to have been transferred to St Mary of Bethany from St Peters, but an objection from St Peters was upheld and Barnsbury

View from York Road Feb 1956.

remained with them. St Peters had been holding services in Barnsbury School for some time and maintained that St Marks was soon to be upgraded to a church and a new road was to be built to link Barnsbury with Westfield. This road was Bonsey Close, but it never did cross the Hoe Stream to link the two communities. St Marys objection was based on the two principals listed above also citing the number of local people visiting the vicarage, which was then on Wych Hill, for baptism and marriage, assuming that they lived in St Mary of Bethany parish.

In the 1960's St Marys made representations with regard to having Barnsbury transferred and were told that there was a proposal to create a new parish out of St Johns and St Peters to take in Barnsbury, Mayford, Westfield and Sutton Green. This did not materialise. Finally on 1st November 1975 Barnsbury was transferred to St Mary of Bethany, and no's 1-7 on the south side of Turnoak Avenue, which included St Peter's vicarage, were transferred to St Peter's.

The latest change to the St Mary of Bethany parish boundary took place in January 2002. A Pastoral Measure was introduced by which St Peters became 'The South Woking Team Ministry' with a Rector and a Vicar. As a small part of this measure nos 1-7 Turnoak Avenue were transferred back to St Marys because St Peters vicarage had been relocated away from Turnoak Avenue.

See page 89 for map.

The chancel with the sanctuary curtains removed. In the foreground the ends of the two Second World War memorial rails can be seen.

Mrs Hall, front left, Joan Hall's mother, talking to the Handsfords family at the Mount Hermon Road end c 1951.

Mount Hermon Road c1951. Note the original lamp post. The lamp on the top was later changed to a modern unit.

Both Sides Of The Bridge

*World War 2
from the
Magazines &
PCC Minutes.*

The accounts before the war started were in deficit and did not improve during hostilities.

Due to black-out restrictions - not showing light at night - the evening services were held in the Kingsway Hall.

29th January 1940

It was hoped to hold evening services in the church from Easter. Black-out materials for the Kingsway hall cost £5 9s 2d.(£5 46p)

2nd April 1940

A new Economy Committee recommended choir boys are not paid until after a probation period.

Gardener for ½ day instead of 1 day.

A voluntary organist to be obtained.

Reduction in Spring Cleaning.

Dispense with organ tuning.

Kingsway Hall Committee to look at increasing hire charges.

6th November 1941

An emergency meeting to discuss protecting the east window against possible air raid damage.

Removal and storage would be £125 but after much discussion it was agreed that wood be fixed to inside and outside and sandbags or corrugated iron inside at a cost of £25-30.

The blacking-out of the Kingsway Hall was reported as being so unsatisfactory that the police had forbidden the use of the hall till it had been remedied. It was agreed to black out half the windows permanently and to obtain curtains for the rest at a cost of possibly £4.

4th February 1941

Economies had saved £40 but the price of coal had gone up.

The Kingsway Hall had increased booking income from the   Education Committee for schools which had used the hall for part of the year.

15th April 1941 APCM

In the absence of Mr Langtree the vicar reported an increase of 1 to 498 on the Electoral Roll. The roll had started 1940 at 480 and went up to 481 in 1942 and 506 in 1942. There was no revision in 1943 but 1944 showed a dramatic drop to 262.

A letter was received from a specialist

company suggesting that the lightning conductor be tested at a cost of £1 5s 0d. (£1 25p) No action to be taken. *(Could this have been an early example of a 'mail shot'?)*

The accounts show repairs due to bomb damage of £6 12s 0d. (£6 60p)

11th August 1942

A special meeting convened at the request of the bishop to discuss his proposal of renewal among Christians was followed by taking the Bishops letter to every house. His concern was a need for urgency of action on the part of the church in view of the background of national sin and of the impact which should have upon the country.

2nd March 1943

Miss Thorne said that the notice board outside the Kingsway Hall needed stronger bolts. *(Life, to some extent, really did carry on as usual during the war.)*

Dec 1943

Neville Wade died in an accident. He sung in the choir and played the organ in the Kingsway Hall. He is remembered on the WW II memorial. *(His initials are carved in the choir stalls!)*

Flight Lieutenant Reginald Lowne was awarded the DFC. *(His brother was killed and is remembered on the WW II memorial.)*

Sgt Navigator Peter Smith baled out over enemy territory, escaped through a neutral country and arrived home after three months. *(He also was a choir member.)*

Nov 1944

Mr West has been able to arrange some of the lights in the church so as to satisfy the authorities, and Sunday evening services are now held at 6.30 at St Marys. The evening services in the hall are therefore discontinued.

July 1945

Our church is still unfinished and is part shabbily furnished. Many chairs are in bad condition.

FOR GOD. FOR KING. AND FOR COUNTRY.

NAMES OF THOSE CONNECTED WITH THIS
CHURCH OF ST. MARY OF BETHANY
WHO FELL DURING THE WAR OF 1914-1919.

BACON,J.L.	HAMILTON,H.O.	RYDE,J.T.
BELBECK.J.H.	HARMAN.A.	SAUNDERS,J.R.S.
CARR,A.	HOMERSHAM,A.J.	SAVORY,M.J.
DRUERY,D.V.	LOMAX,T.H.	SAVORY,E.H.
GREENFIELD,G.H.	LOVELOCK,A.A.G.	TIDD,E.G.
GRIPPER,E.C.	MARSH,A.L.	WALKER,F.C.
HADDOW,W.P.	NESS,A.	WOOLF,W.F.
HAMILTON,G.de C.	PEAKE,W.F.C.	

"FAITHFUL UNTIL DEATH"

The Great War 1st World War memorial plaque.

The Great War Memorial, top, and 2nd World War memorial which was moved to this position in 2004. Originally the name plates were fitted onto a pair of kneeling rails.

The 2nd World War memorial plaque.

THESE KNEELING RAILS ARE
DEDICATED TO THE GLORY OF
GOD AND IN GRATEFUL AND
AFFECTIONATE MEMORY OF
THOSE FROM THIS CHURCH AND
PARISH WHO GAVE THEIR LIVES
IN THE SECOND WORLD WAR
1939-1945

The alabaster plaque installed in the north wall records those parishioners who gave their lives during the First World War 1914-1918, known before the 2nd World War as the Great War,- the war to end all wars..

Christ Church, St Pauls and St Marys all had plaques. The plaque at St Mary of Bethany was unveiled at the 11.00am service on 17th October 1920 by the vicar Rev Price-Devereaux. The Christ Church Memorial includes 232 names from the whole parish.

Bacon J L
The Rev JOHN LIONEL BACON
Chaplain who died on Sunday 1st December 1918. Age
Son of William and Catherine Bacon, of Friar's Hall, Hadleigh, Suffolk; husband of Charlotte Bacon, of 30, Rosemont Rd., Acton, London. C.M.S. Missionary working among Chinese labour battalions.
Cemetery: St Marie Cemetery Le Havre, Seine-Maritime,
John Bacon was St Mary's 'own missionary' who had returned home from China to offer his services as chaplain for the war. His wife Charlotte Bacon was also a missionary in China and for many years organist at St Mary's..

Belbek J H
JOHN HENRY BELBECK Private 41/48 7th Bn., Northamptonshire Regiment who died on Sunday 15th December 1918. Age 19.
Son of John H. and Sophie Belbeck, of Clare Cottage, Goldsworth Rd., Woking.
Cemetery: Niederzwehren Cemetery, Kassel, Hessen, Germany

Carr A
ARTHUR CLUNES HOOPER CARR Lieutenant Royal Engineers
who died on Monday 15 February 1915
Cemetery: Ypres (Menin Gate) Memorial, Ieper, West-Vlaanderen,

Druery D V
DUDLEY VICTORY DRUERY Second Lieutenant 13th Kensington Bn., London Regiment who died on Friday 18th October 1918.
Cemetery: St Sever Cemetery Extension, Rouen, Seine-Maritime,

Greenfield D G H
GERALD HENRY GREENFIELD Second Lieutenant "B" Bty. 242nd Bde., Royal Field Artillery who died on Friday 17th August 1917. Age 20.
Son of Mrs. M. Greenfield, of Edenmore, Woking, and the late Henry Greenfield.
Cemetery: Lijssenthoek Military Cemetery, Poperinge, West-Vlaanderen, Belgium

Gripper E C
EDWARD CUTBUSH GRIPPER Captain 7th Bn., King's Own Yorkshire Light Infantry who died on Wednesday 5th December 1917. Age 29.
Son of John Edward and Annie Ellen Gripper, of Barnes, London; husband of Ruby K. Gripper, of Ward's Cross, Hurst, Twyford, Berks.
Cemetery: Etaples Military Cemetery, Pas de Calais,

Haddow W P

WALTER PETER HADDOW Corporal G/1720 7th Bn., The Queen's (Royal West Surrey Regt.) who died on Thursday 13th July 1916. Age 23.
Son of Peter and Emily Haddow, of Starhill, Woking, Surrey. Cemetery: Thiepval Memorial, Somme, France.

Hamilton G de C

GERALD de COURCY HAMILTON Lieutenant Royal Navy
He died on 10th February 1922 aged 22 at the Palace Hotel, Montana S/Sierre, Valais, Switzerland. Gerald did not die during the war. The style of lettering on the memorial is slightly different indicating that it was added later. He was born at home, Ringrone, Guildford Road, Woking on 1st August 1899. His father was a solicitor and his mother is mentioned in a Christ Church magazine around 1900. Gerald trained at the submarine training base, HMS Dolphin, in Gosport. In 1918 he was a Sub Lieutenant at HMS Dolphin and in 1920 a Sub Lieutenant on HMS Lucia a submarine depot ship in Devon, possibly Plymouth. Did his training take him into hostilities at the end of the war? His death was registered 20 months later at the Geneva Consulate. Overseas death certificates do not record cause of death. One suggestion is that he contracted TB and had gone to Switzerland to recuperate but if so why was he added to the memorial? He does not appear on the Christ Church or town centre memorials or in The Commonwealth War Graves Commission records.

Hamilton H O

HERBERT OTHO HAMILTON Lieutenant 12th Bn., Northumberland Fusiliers who died on Saturday 25th September 1915.
Son of Rev WFT Hamilton Vicar of Cromer, Norfolk. Remembered with honour Loos Memorial, Pas de Calais, France. William Hamilton paid for the land and the building of St Mary of Bethany Church. Herbert joined up in August 1914 after seeing the 'Your Country Needs You!' Poster. He had been helping his father with a beach mission at Cromer during August. Herbert was commissioned as a Second Lieutenant and posted to the 4th Officers Training Battalion at Berkhampstead where he met 20 year old Muriel Wakley. They were married on 28th January at Tring Parish Church. The 21st division crossed to France between 2nd and 13th September 1915 and after lengthy forced marches were kept in reserve at Loos. It was too far from the front line to be a useful reinforcement and was sent into action on the 25th. His body was never found. A comrade said "He was a splendid officer, the first man to go over the parapet when the order was given to charge".

Harman A

ARTHUR HARMAN Private SD/1048 11th Bn., Royal Sussex Regiment who died on Sunday 3rd September 1916. Age 19.
Son of George Richard and Alice Harman, of 271, Mount Pleasant Rd., Hastings Cemetery: Thieval Memorial, Somme, France

Homersham A J

ALFRED JONES HOMERSHAM   Lieutenant Royal Flying Corps, formerly London Regiment
who died on Monday 18th February 1918. Age 25.
Son of Alfred and Sophia Homersham, of "Lampeter", Mount Hermon Rd., Woking, Surrey; husband of Phyllis Olive Homersham.
Cemetery: Gorre British and Indian Cemetery, Pas de Calais, France

Lomax T H
THOMAS HENRY LOMAX Lance Corporal G/1721 7th Bn., The Queen's (Royal West Surrey Regt.) who died on Saturday 1st July 1916.
Cemetery: Thiepval Memorial, Somme, France

Lovelock A A G
ALBERT ARTHUR LOVELOCK Airman 2nd Class 43584 RFC. attd. 6th Siege Bty., Royal Garrison Artillery
who died on Tuesday 31st July 1917. Cemetery: Cite Bonjean Military Cemetery, Armentieres, Nord, France

Marsh A L
ARTHUR LEONARD MARSH Corporal 550104 (1197). "A" Coy. 1st/16th Bn., London Regt (Queen's Westminster Rifles)
who died on Saturday 1st July 1916. Age 23.
Son of Joseph William and Alice Martha Marsh, of 6, Claremont Avenue, Woking,
Cemetery: Thiepval Memorial, Somme, France

Ness A
JAMES CHARLES ALEXANDER NESS Lieutenant Bedfordshire Regiment
Who died on Sunday 27th June 1915.
Cemetery: Le Touret Memorial, Pas de Calais, France

Peake W F C
WILLIAM FRANCIS COPSON PEAKE Lieutenant 1st Bn, The Queen's (Royal West Surrey Regt.) who died on Friday 7th July 1916. Age 29.
Son of Mr. F. C. Peake and Mrs. A. J. Peake, of Locksley. Woking, Native of Horsell.
Cemetery: St. Sever Cemetery, Rouen, Seine-Maritime, France

Ryde JT
JOHN TITCOMBE RYDE Second Lieutenant 1st Bn., Bedfordshire Regiment attd. 12th Bn. , Gloucestershire Regiment
who died on Tuesday 8th May 1917. Cemetery: Arras Memorial, Pas de Calais, France

Saunders JRS
JAMES OSCAR REGINALD STUART SAUNDERS Second Lieutenant 100th Sqdn., Royal Air Force
who died on Monday 21st October 1918. Age 20. Son of George Saunders, OBE, LLD and Gertrude Saunders, of Pontsarn, Woking, Surrey.
Cemetery: Niederzwehren Cemetery, Kassel, Hessen, Germany

Savory MJ
MAURICE JEFFERY SAVORY Captain 9th Bn., Duke of Wellington's (West Riding Regt.)
who died on Saturday 3rd February 1917. Age 22. Son of Ernest J. C. and Madeline Savory, of The Red Lodge, Woking.
Enlisted, Sept., 1914. Severely wounded, April, 1916. Returned to France, Jan., 1917. Cemetery: Grove Town Cemetery, Meaulte, Somme, France

Savory E H

ERNEST HARLEY SAVORY Second Lieutenant 7th Bn., The Queen's (Royal West Surrey Regt.)
who died on Friday 10th August 1917. Age 20. Son of Ernest Jeffery Charles and Madeline Savory, of The Red Lodge, Woking.
Cemetery: Ypres (Menin Gate) Memorial, Ieper, West-Vlaanderen, Belgium

Tidd E G

ERNEST GEORGE TIDD Captain 6th Bn., Highland Light Infantry
who died on Sunday 13th June 1915. Cemetery: Helles Memorial, Turkey

Walker F C

FREDERIC CHARLES WALKER Second Lieutenant 8th Bn., Suffolk Regiment
who died on Thursday 25th November 1915. Age 33.
Son of E. J. and Jane Walker, of Sloane St., Chelsea, London; husband of Margaret Walker, of "Easedale," 66, York Rd., Woking.
Cemetery: Albert Communal Cemetery Extension, Somme, France

Woolf W F

W F WOOLF Second Lieutenant 7th Bn., King's Shropshire Light Infantry
who died on Wednesday 27th March 1918. Age 20.
Son of Maj. and Mrs. H. G. Woolf, of "Simley," Woking, Surrey. Cemetery: Wailly Orchard Cemetry, Pas de Calais, France
His wife Mrs B du T Woolf of 19 Mount Hermon Road died on 15th June 1963. The family began to attend St Marys during WW1. Mrs Woolfe provided flowers near the war memorial after her son's death. W F Woolf had two sisters May and Sybil.

By February 1948 only five names had been put forward for a memorial. The matter was raised again in June 1951 and a new request for names was publicised. At the July 3rd PCC meeting a lack of interest was noted. Adding a tablet below the WWI memorial was discussed but by December the erection of two kneeling rails had been agreed and costed at £50 approx. The dedication was set for June 22nd 1952 but was rescheduled for Sunday 9th Nov 1952. The RR C E Curzon former Bishop of Exeter performed the dedication and preached. During the reordering of 1994 they were moved from their original position at the front of the nave seating to their current position at either side of the dais and restained a darker colour to match other new woodwork. In 2003 the rails were removed and stored. The nameplates were mounted on a wooden plaque and fixed to the wall below the First World War memorial.

Sgt S E Bradshaw RAF
SYDNEY EDWARD BRADSHAW Sergeant 1168179 W.Op./Air Gnr. 61 Sqdn., Royal Air Force Volunteer Reserve
Lancaster squadron based at Syerston Nottinghamshire and St Eval Cornwall.
Died on Tuesday 23rd June 1942. Age 20.
Son of Oliver and Lily Margaret Bradshaw, of Polegate, Sussex.
Possibly of Minera Bonsey Lane in 1947.
Cemetery: Sage War Cemetery, Oldenburg, Niedersachsen, Germany.

Flt Lt J F Lown RAF
JOHN FREDERICK LOWN Flight Lieutenant 66022 248 Sqdn., R A F Volunteer Reserve. Based at Banff Aberdeenshire.
Died after his Mosquito was hit by flak during attack on merchant ships in Flekkefjord on Sunday 31st December 1944. Age 24.
Son of Frederick William and Lilian Jane Lown of 37, York Road, Woking.
Cemetery: Runneymede Memorial, Surrey.

Flt Sgt H F Moroni RAF
HUBERT FRANK MORONI Sergeant 1389016 15 Sqdn., Royal Air Force Volunteer Reserve. Lancaster Squadron based at Wyton Mildenhall.
Died on Sunday 20th February 1944 aged 21 during Battle of Berlin.
Son of Frank Moroni and Jane Elizabeth Moroni of 147, Goldsworth Rd, Woking.
Cemetery: Berlin 1939-1945 War Cemetery, Berlin, Germany.

Lieut G N Noll RN

GORDON MAURICE NOLL Lieutenant   H.M. Submarine Untamed, Royal
Navy. Lost with all hands during working-up trial. Failed to surface off Sansa
Island, South of Kintyre.
Died on Sunday 30th May 1943. Age 25.   Son of Maurice George and
Gwendoline Elizabeth Noll. Husband of Diana Constance Joan Noll, of Lower
Saltram, Devon.
Cemetery: Dunoon Cemetery, Argyllshire.

Lieut E B Talbot RN

EDWARD BARTLE TALBOT Lieutenant H.M. Submarine Snapper, Royal
Navy.   Lost with all hands south west of Ushant after German minesweepers
depth charge attack. Died on Wednesday 12th February 1941. Age 25.
Son of Vice-Admiral Sir Cecil Ponsonby Talbot, KCB, KBE, DSO, and Lady
Talbot, of Orchard Mains, Woking, Surrey.
Cemetery: Portsmouth Naval Memorial, Hampshire.

Lieut F R G Talbot RN

FRANCIS ROBERT CECIL TALBOT Lieutenant   H.M. Submarine Thames,
Royal Navy.
Lost presumed mined off coast of Norway 22/23 July 1940.
Died on Saturday 3rd August 1940. Age 26.
Son of Vice-Admiral Sir Cecil Ponsonby Talbot, KCB, KBE, DSO, and Lady
Talbot, of Orchard Mains, Woking, Surrey.
Cemetery: Portsmouth Naval Memorial, Hampshire.

Lieut R H Scales RNVR

REGINALD HERBERT SCALES Lieutenant   H.M.S. Fiji., Royal Naval
Volunteer Reserve who died on Friday 23rd May 1941. Age 32.
Died in enemy aircraft fire during Battle of Crete HMS Fiji sunk on 22nd May
1941. Husband of Trina Scales. Possibly son of A W Scales of Culver Cottage,
Horsell Vale.
Cemetery: Portsmouth Naval Memorial, Hampshire.

Lieut Com R M Sowdon RN

RONALD MONTAGUE HAIGH SOWDON Lieut-Commander in Despatches.
R.N. H.M.S. Dunedin, Cruiser 4850 tons Royal Navy.
Torpedoed by U124 in South Atlantic. Died on Monday 24th November 1941.
Age 41. Survivors included 4 officers and 64 ratings.
Ship visited by Duke of Windsor and Mrs Simpson in Bermuda.
Son of Henry Lucy Sowdon and Catherine Edith Sowdon; husband of Edith
Monica Sowdon of Horsell, Woking.
Cemetery: Portsmouth Naval Memorial Hampshire
His wife Monica was a regular worshipper at St Marys and lived in Turnoak
Avenue until she died in 2004. A book has been written about HMS Dunedin -
Blood on the Water.

Sgt F H Stevens Home Guard

FRANK HENRY STEVENS MM Serjeant 1st (Surrey) Bn., Home Guard.
Died during exercises on Sunday 26th January 1941. Age 55.
He was awarded the Military Medal during WW1.   Son of Arthur and Elizabeth
Stevens; husband of Lily Edith Stevens, possibly of The Cottage, Goldsworth
Road, Woking.
Cemetery: Brookwood Cemetery, Surrey. All Souls Avenue, Grave 202860.

C I N Wade RAFVR

NEVILLE WADE   Aircraftman 1st Class 1236350 Royal Air Force Volunteer
Reserve.
Died in an accident on Wednesday 10 November 1943 . Age 21.
Son of Timothy and Winifred Wade, of 42, Westfield Road, Woking.
Cemetery: St Peters Church, Old Woking. Plot 4. Grave 1458.

Raymond Lee's story with apologies to W S Gilbert. A parody of Captain Corcoran's song from 'HMS Pinafore'.

I was a Plymouth Brother at the Varsity
    of Oxford where I took an Arts Degree.
At Bristol read Theology so I could
    be a Vicar in the C of E.

When I came down with cap and gown
    I went to Tooting up in London Town.
With the firm intent whatever might be
    that I'd become a Vicar in the C of E.

At Tooting as an ordinand
    I had laid on me the Bishop's hand.
I learned the collects and the Liturgy
    and now I am a Vicar in the C of E.

I cane to Woking in '62
    to a parish in a town that is really 'U'.
Here our family increased to three
    with the birth in '63 of little Timothy.

I ran Top Gear with youthful glee
    and the very next week the B.B.C.
sent down a little man to interview me
    and now I an a Vicar who's been on T.V.

In processional hymns I walk in last
    I get very cross if the choir walk fast.
I take each step with dignity
    befitting of a Vicar in the C of E.

I chair the meetings of the P.C.C.
    they last front 8 until eternity.
But e'en eternity is all too short
    for any business other than the Vicar's report.

In the Parish of St. Mary of Bethany
    I find a nice living that has suited me
Here we found prosperity
    and now we are a two car family.

Heading notices in church I find such a bore
    So I put 'em in a letter and preach five minutes more.
The Epistle of Paul to Timothy
    has nothing on the letters sent from Raymond Lee.

The Kingsway Hall
Land Purchased c1899 for £250
Built 1911
Cost £750
Burnt Down 17/05/1972
Land Sold

   A new Mission Hall - The Kingsway Hail was opened and dedicated by the Bishop of Guildford on 2nd March 1911. Prior to the Kingsway Hall a room was hired for church work in Mr Broderick's house, 49 Royal Oak Road. Also Rev Mowll held an after service meeting for railwaymen and their families at a railwayman's house in Wilfred Street. William Hamilton purchased the land for the Kingsway Hall when Oaks Farm was sold for building plots. Oaks Farm covered an area from Goldsworth Road to the railway and the full length of the Kingsway. In 1914 at least a third was still for sale at reduced prices. *'The price being nearly 50% lower than it was a few years ago'.*

Kingsway Hall plot

SOLD TITHE FREE.
FREE CONVEYANCES

LAND TAX REDEEMED

= OAKS FARM ESTATE, WOKING. =

POINTS FOR YOUR CONSIDERATION.

A full double page spread advertisement from a Woking News and Mail supplement celebrating 20 years and 1000 issues in Woking.

Friday February 20th 1914.

The building served a great many purposes during its 51 year life. It was, like St Mary of Bethany church, part of Christ Church Parish until 1923. As well as St Mary's activities Goldsworth School, now the Surrey History Centre, used it as a lunchtime pupil's canteen. An agreement with Surrey County Council dated 20th March 1958 allowed for the use of the hall as a canteen for school meals. It lists all the fixtures and fittings of the hall. The caretaker around this time was Mrs Champion who lived almost opposite the hall. She had a Morris Minor with a registration number which always caused amusement with silly school boys - NOT ***
- but of course it was!

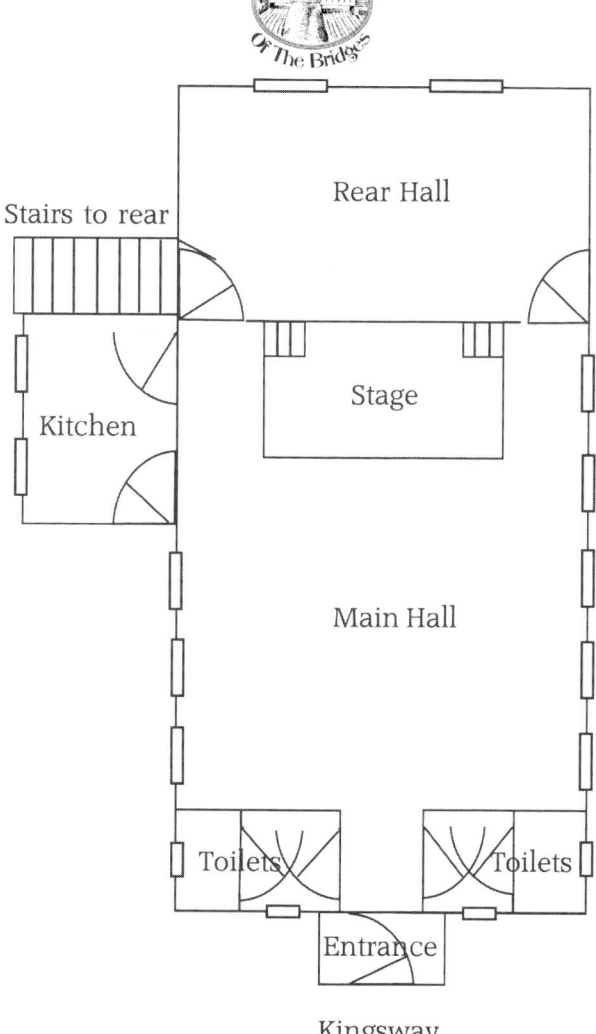

A sketch, drawn from memory and photos, showing the approximate layout of the Kingsway Hall.

During the Second World War evening services were held in the Kingsway hall because it was too difficult to black out the windows of the church.

Sunday Schools were held there on Sunday afternoons. The Mother's Union held their meetings on Monday afternoons. It was used for Harvest Suppers, and Youth Fellowship held meetings inside and made great use of the ground outside, (it would be incorrect to call it grass), as did Scouts, Cubs, Guides and Brownies. My parents were both Youth Club members and remember playing tennis on the two courts behind the hall, so the grass must have been very tidy at one time.

The Kingsway Hall consisted of 2 rooms, a large hall at the front with a stage and a smaller hall behind. A kitchen, which was very basic, was built on the side.

The smaller rear hall, 24' x 20', was an extension built in 1927 due to the increasing number of uses demanded of the hall. At the same time the toilets were added, the kitchen enlarged and probably the rear stairs were added. The extension was designed by a St Mary's member Mr M E Walker and built by Mr W J Drowley of Bath Road. When the extension was dedicated it was still only known that the land had been donated by 'parishioner'.

A YCF group waiting for transport for an outing, probably to Wittering. The front elevation of the Kingsway Hall is just visible. c 1964.

A Sunday School class in progress in the main hall, or they having a picnic?

At 4.50pm on Wednesday 17th May 1972 a fire severely damaged the hall, before appliances from Woking and Guildford arrived. A teacloth hanging over the cooker was believed to be the cause of the fire.

A view of the rear elevation of the Kingsway Hall taken just after the fire.

You may have seen in some older churches that a number of pews are arranged in an enclosed square with an access door, similar to a theatre box. These, and more conventional pews, were set aside for the wealthy families of the parish - The Lord of the Manor etc. The household staff would also join the families for the services. A fee was payable to the church for this privilege and was known as Pew Rent, also called sittings. This usually went to the incumbent's stipend.

When St Mary of Bethany church was consecrated sittings were still the norm. William Hamilton stipulated that:-

> '...half the church should be free, the dividing line being east to west as it is in Christ Church'

This arrangement was quite unusual. The usual arrangement was for the rented pews to be spread across the front of the aisles, with the free seats behind.

Mr & Mrs Fred Hutchins lived in Croydon when their home was bombed during WW2. They moved to Woking and bought a house at 150 Goldsworth Road. Mr Hutchins was asked if he would like to rent their seats and William Hamilton's unusual seating arrangement was mentioned. The rented centre aisle had strips of carpet and kneelers installed some years previously. Fred Hutchins said that this was against the spirit of William Hamilton's gift that at all seats should be equal. He suggested that carpet and kneelers were placed in the free seats. After some thought and discussion it was agreed to remove every other row of carpet and kneelers and place them in every other row of the free seats. Finances were in very poor shape during the war and the added expense of purchasing extra carpet was not possible. The Hutchins then rented their seats.

The practise of sittings started to die out with the end of the Great War. Many family heirs had been killed during the war and large houses were sold. The traditional level of household staff was drastically reduced.

Crockfords Clerical Directory 1904 listing for Christ Church shows that out of a total income of £348, £264 was received from pew rents. In 1939 you could still rent your seat for one guinea (£! 5p) a year although moves were afoot to abolish the practice even though it was a good steady source of income.

At St Marys a small brass frame was attached to the top rail of the chair into which was inserted a card with the occupants name.

From a St Mary of Bethany magazine of 1946:-

'PEW RENTS are a decreasing factor in the income of all churches, and although there is still a sincere difference of opinion on the matter they are generally considered an anachronism. There would be much to be said for having reserved pews if it was still the general custom for families to worship together regularly; sadly this is not so; and most people can ensure sufficient seats together for themselves and their friends by being in good time for the services.

There are now only about twenty-five 'Pew-renters' at St. Marys, and the seats so let are clearly marked and numbered at both ends of the row. No further seats are being let and some who hold seats have decided to free them and to pay an equal amount yearly into the general funds. At present Pew Rents are paid direct into the Vicar's Stipend Fund.

Meanwhile those holding seats are asked to occupy them at least by the time the second bell stops ringing; those not holding seats are asked kindly not to occupy named seats until after the second bell. It will help if Sidesmen note this rule in seating the congregation, especially when the church is well filled. The second bell stops ringing usually about two minutes before the service is due to commence.'

*Magazine
April 1931.*

Wych Hill

The first vicarage was purchased from Mr Henry Charles Newton for £2500 on 27th July 1925. It was on the corner of

York Road and what was then called Whitstreet Lane, now Wych Hill Lane. The house named Carlton was built by Tarrant in 1906 on two plots, nos 61 and 62 of West Hill Park Estate for Mr Duka a chancery barrister.

Two reports were written concerning the purchase of the house for use as a vicarage. One by Mr A L Ryde a *"past president of the surveyors institution"* for St Mary of Bethany and one by Caröe and Passmore for the church commissioners. They reported that it was not up to the Church Commissioners requirements as it had *"only two sitting rooms and no housemaids pantry"* although there was *"a motor house of temporary construction."*

On 14th June 1961 a narrow piece of ground 5'- 0" wide, (1.5m), was sold to Mrs M K Burgess of 122 York Road; on the left in the upper photo.

The vicarage and grounds were sold for £44,000 on 11th July 1974 to A & J Simmons Homes Ltd for development. They built 2 houses in York Road as nos 124 and 126, and converted the vicarage into eight flats. The old vicarage is now named St Mary's House. The long garden extended into York Road and was used for many garden parties, sales, teas etc. It also had a tennis court which could be hired. This seemed to pay its own way with a new perimeter netting installed one year followed by a playing net the following year.

The first vicarage in Wych Hill. The two new houses built in the back garden are just visible on the left.

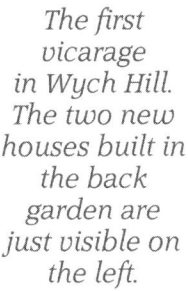

Current vicarage in West Hill Road.

West Hill Road

A new vicarage, the current one, was purchased in West Hill Road when Rev Norgate became vicar. This house was previously known as Rostrevor.

CHERTSEY ROAD.

THE MOSQUE.

WESLEYAN CHURCH.

PINEWOOD AT WOODHAM.

WOKING

VIEW ON CANAL

WYCH HILL.

This very rare postcard of Woking postmarked 8.15pm March 27th 1908 shows the house which became the vicarage in Wych Hill, bottom right.

The text reads as follows:-

The new church must have been St Mary of Bethany. It was only six months old in March 1908. The Wesleyan church on the postcard was built in 1899. The post card was found in Malmesbury in 2005.

Dear E

Hope this will find you well.

I have sent mother a postcard with the new church I went to last Sunday morning.

Ask her from me to let you see it.

From Doll

A ground floor flat at 155 York Road was rented in 1961 on a three year lease from Miss V G Norris, who lived upstairs, for curate Colin Bedford followed by Robert Hope. Miss Norris was one of the original worshippers from 1907 when St Marys was dedicated. She was also on the first PCC after St Marys became a separate parish in 1923

When Miss Norris died in 1964 the house was sold and left Robert Hope and his new wife Selby née Smith homeless, so a house was purchased for £3600 at 7 Wilbury Road. This was used for many Youth Fellowship meetings.

Two houses are currently owned by St Marys and are either let or house St Mary's staff.

7 Wilbury Road.

155 York Road.

St Mary of Bethany current houses.

*The East
Window.
See page 38.*

*The
Backcloth.
See
page 56.*

Not strictly St Marys but this post box outside the car park in Mount Hermon Road is older than the church. Have you ever looked at it? It's Victorian. A photograph of c1901 shows the post box, the lamp post and the houses. The lamp post is original but the light on the top is newer.

The Reredos. See page 40.

Both Sides
Of The Bridges

St Mary of Bethany Parish boundary changes from 1924 to 2002. See page 64 for full story of the parish.

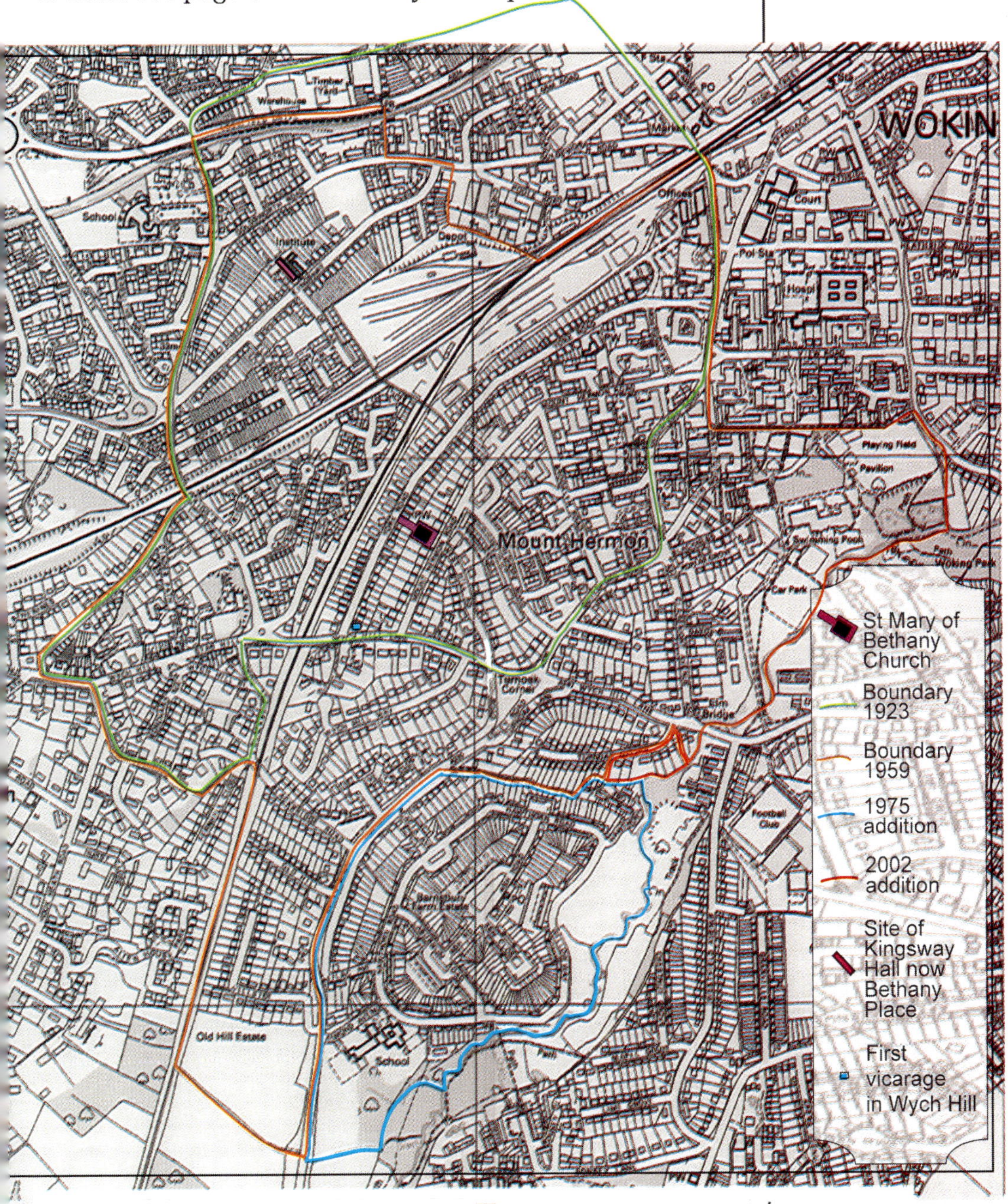

WOKIN

Mount Hermon

St Mary of Bethany Church

Boundary 1923

Boundary 1959

1975 addition

2002 addition

Site of Kingsway Hall now Bethany Place

First vicarage in Wych Hill

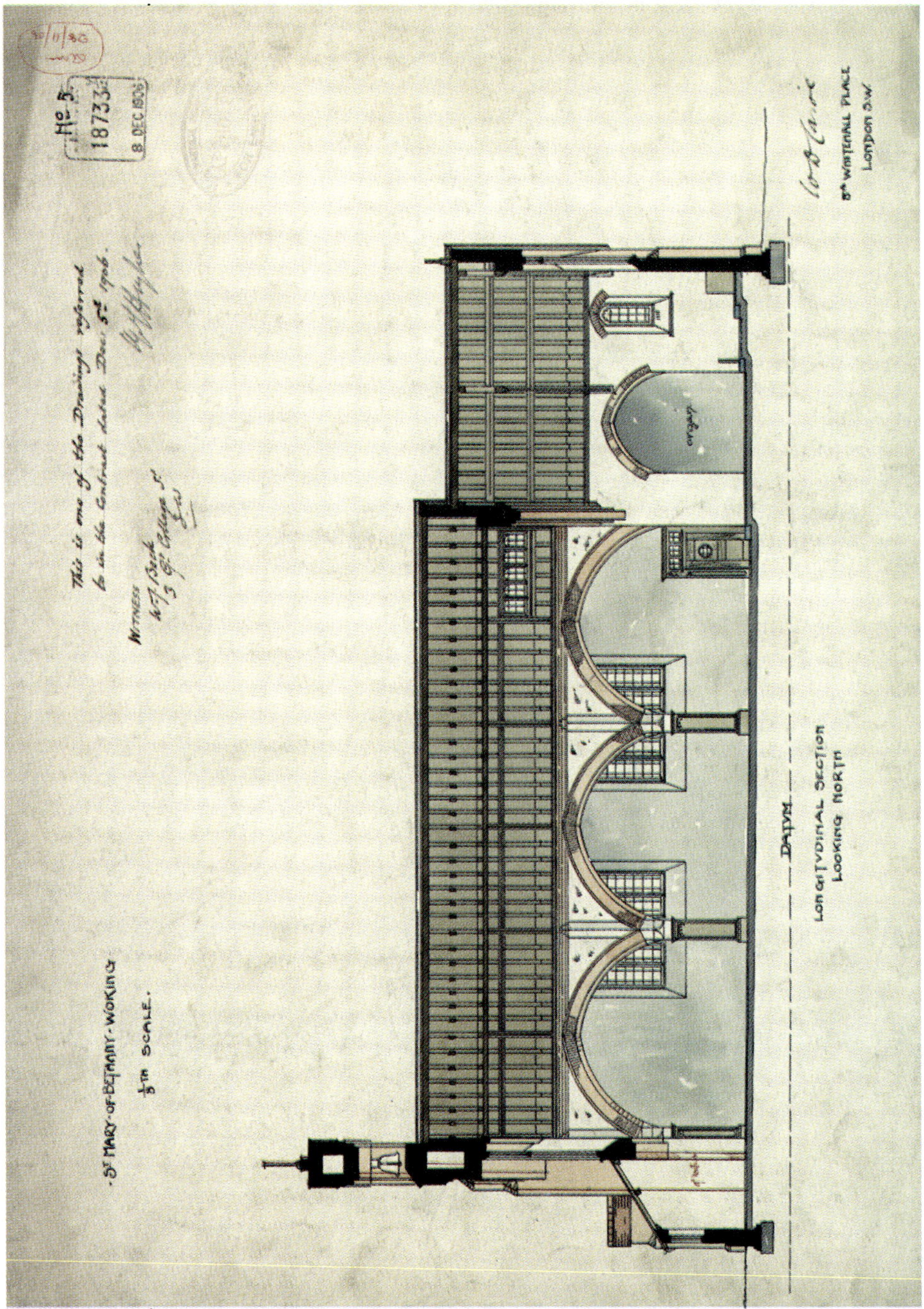

ST MARY-OF-BETHANY · WOKING.
⅛ᵗʰ SCALE.

DATUM

LONGITUDINAL SECTION
LOOKING NORTH

One of W D Caröe's original coloured contract drawings. This sectional view is looking north through the chancel and nave. It is signed by E C Hughes the contractor.

Part 3
The People

Elsie Wright, born and brought up in a very affluent home, cheerfully went to work in a factory in the early nineteen-forties, when conditions made it necessary for everyone to make some contribution to the war effort.

Rev Stanley William Phillips MA
03/03/1924 - 02/11/1944

C M S Organising Secretary for
Diocese of Exeter and Truro
1913 - 1918

Vicar St James Teignmouth Devon

Rev Jack Edward Marshall MA
27/01/1945 - 21/07/1953

St John the Evangelist Penge
1943 - 1944

Vicar St. Pancras Chichester

Rev Robert Michael Brettell MA
30/11/1953 - 23/03/1962

Curate St Peters Norbiton
1951 - 1953

Vicar Christ Church, Clifton, Bristol,
1962-1973

Rev Raymond John Lee MA
15/05/1962 - 17/07/1970

Vicar St Johns Muswell Hill
1959 - 1962

Canon St Lukes Gt Crosby,
Liverpool 1970 - 1982

Rev Norman George Norgate MA
25/01/1971 - 1983

Vicar St Peters Bexley Heath
1963 - 1970

Vicar St James Tunbridge Wells

Rev Roger Derbridge MA
16/04/1984 - 09/2004

Team Vicar St Philemon w St Gabriel
Toxteth

Retired on leaving 09/2004

Rev Stephen Robert Beak
  10/03/2005 -

Curate Howell Hill 1997

NSM* St Mary of Bethany 2001-2005

Current vicar

The procedure for appointing a new incumbent stipulates that he/she cannot be chosen until the previous one has resigned and moved on. The ensuing time without an incumbent is known as an Interregnum. Hence the gaps in the dates above.

The entries are arranged as follows-
 -Name
 -Date starting and leaving St Marys
 -Position held before St Marys
 -Position held after leaving St Marys

*NSM non stipendary minister

Curates

Rev.William Hugh Andrew, MA,	asst. curate 1958-1961
Rev.Colin Michael Bedford,	asst. curate 1961-1963
Rev.Robert Hope, B.Sc.,	asst. curate 1963-1966
Rev.Dale Raymond Oldham,	asst. curate 1967-1970

Missionaries

These are some of the people from St Marys who went abroad as missionaries

Daphne Richardson (Evans) - South American Missionary Society; sailed to Valpariso in Chile in October 1964
Sheila Jones - Lahore
Rosamunde Oxlade
Joan Hall - Rushere Hospital Uganda
Malcolm & Ann Jones - 1965 left for Singapore with China Inland Mission Overseas Missionary Fellowship
Muriel Martin - Uganda
Phyllis Russell
Jean Harrison - Canada teaching
Bob & Gale McLeod - Central Europe

Ordained

These are some of the people from St Marys who have been ordained

Richard Bedford	Alex Martin	John Baggs
Robert Warren	Gordon Oram	John Coombs
Gordon Percy	Geoffery Goater	Richard Cowan
John Richards	Richard Worsfold	Robert Innes
Andrew Facey	Leigh Machell	Fiona Windsor
Des Williamson	Lorelli Hilliard	Ray Marks

1906/07	Mr A W Smyth	1965-68	Mr M D Bolton
	Mr E Collins		Mr F J Heather
1907/08	Mr E Collins	1969-73	Mr J Bednall
	Mr J A Ness		Mr D Hughes
1908-13	Mr A J Ness	1973-75	Dr D Hughes
1913-17	Mr B Leach		Dr D R M Marks
1917-24	Mr C E Watkins	1975-77	Dr D R M Marks
			Mr D Methold
St Mary's becomes a parish		1977-79	Mr D Methold
			Mr A Mitchell
1924/25	Mr R Atherton	1979-82	Mr P Scott
	Mr C E Watkins		Dr D R M Marks
1925/26	Mr R Atherton	1982-84	Mr M Bolton
	?		Mr P Scott
1926/28	Mr R Atherton	1985/86	Mr M Bolton
	Mr H Allan		Mr G Worsfold
1928-32	Mr R Atherton	1987-89	Cpt P Woodhead
	Col A Wright CBE		Mr G Worsfold
1932-42	Mr M G Noll	1990/91	Mrs P McDonald
	Mr R B Roberts		Cpt P Woodhead
1942/43	Mr R B Roberts	1991/92	Mrs P McDonald
	Mr J Dalrymple		Dr D R M Marks
1943/44	Mr J Dalrymple	1993/94	Dr D R M Marks
	Mr M Eyre Walker		Mr J Pout
1945/46	Mr J Dalrymple	1994-96	Dr R Marks
	Mr CHS Lewis		Miss E Daniels
1947-50	Mr J Dalrymple	1996-99	Miss E Daniels
	Mr J R Whiteman		Mr G Musslewhite
1951/52	Mr J Dalrymple	1999/2000	Miss E Daniels
	Mr C Meek/Mr Lane		Mr S Ensoll
1953/54	Mr J Dalrymple	2000/01	Mr S Ensoll
	Mr A S Lane MBE		Mis J Brown
1955-57	Mr J Dalrymple	2001-03	Mr D Price
	Lt Col G Clarke		Mrs J Brown
1958/59	Lt Col G Clarke	2003-05	Mrs J Brown
	Mr P G Warren		Mrs L Pocock
1960-62	Mr P G Warren	2005-07	Mrs L Pocock
	Mr M G Lowe		Mr S Crosland
1963/64	Mr M G Lowe	2007/08	Mr S Crosland
	Mr M D Bolton		Mrs H Brooks

From 1906-1923 when St Marys was a chapel-of-ease to Christ Church deputy wardens were appointed.

Unfortunately there is not enough room to write many of the interesting life stories of St Mary's worshippers but Elsie Wright appears quite often in magazines etc.

Born and brought up in a very affluent home, Elsie Mareurite Wright certainly never expected in her younger days to see the inside of a factory as a worker. When in the early nineteen-forties, conditions made it necessary for everyone to make some contribution to the war effort, Miss Wright cheerfully went to work in a factory.

It was not long before Daisy, as she was usually called, felt that there was a need for Christians who were engaged in various different kinds of work associated with the war effort to gather together for fellowship, prayer and to become more effective witnesses to their fellow workers. At first a small group of Christians involved in Air Raid Patrol gathered in her house for prayer. The vision expanded and at the end of 1942 there were 12 groups in and around Woking meeting primarily for prayer. These early groups banded together under the name Wartime Christian Fellowship.

Miss Wright and her motorcycle.

When the war came to an end, Daisy and others like her returned from industry to their homes. Miss Wright, who never married, felt that the many Christians who normally work in factories and other places in industry and commerce still needed the kind of inspiration and encouragement to witness that a Fellowship such as she had founded could provide. The WCF continued to grow under the new title of Workers Christian Fellowship. An executive committee was formed of which Miss Wright was honorary secretary. This meant in practice that she did all the office work of the Fellowship for many years and attended to all the correspondence from her home.

In 1985 to bring a more up-to-date appeal WCF was renamed Christians at Work.

Such a place

Such a place this is
Where man meets God
And sings His praises.

Where young and old
Are both at home
And play their part.

Where proud new mums
Bring babes for doting
And fears for calming.

Where cocky kids
Can teach their elders
And yet learn grace.

Such a place this is
Where broken hearts find healing
And the downtrodden are lifted up.

Where those who were told that they can't
Now find they can;
And teach others how.

Where the tuneless sing like angels
When God is in their hearts,
And the sad are wrapped in arms that fear no tears.

Such a place this is:
Filled with the blessed and the blessing,
The cared for and the caring,
The annoyed and annoying,
The frustrated and frustrating,
The imperfect and the sinful.

And yet the smiling Saviour looks down on it all,
And makes it right,
And makes us right.

Such a place this is
And I love it.

Simon Harrison 2007

Henry Doughty has kept a file of programmes for the Choir Festivals, Nine Lessons and Carols, and Handel's Messiah for the period when he was organist and choirmaster (1945-1954).

His copy of the programme for the Messiah which was performed at 7.45pm Saturday 29th March 1952 is covered with his interesting handwritten notes.

The weather;

"Thick continuous snow and gale force winds".

The account for the performance shows that expenses were £10.6.6d (£10.33p) and the collection £11.10.4d (£11.52p) giving a credit balance of £1.3.10d (£1.19p).

Expenses were made up as follows: Mr Meeks £9.6.6d (£9.33p) including 30/- (£1.50p) for an advert; Henry Doughty's oboe 2/8d (14p), phone and post 7/10d (39p), Redgrave C. Ch. (Christ Church) 2/0d (10p), lorry driver, chairs etc 7/6d (33p).

The choir totalled 55 including 10 first sopranos, 12 second sopranos, 11 altos, 12 tenors and 10 basses, all named on the back of the programme.

Programme for a performance of Handel's Messiah 29th March 1952.

PARISH CHURCH of St. MARY OF BETHANY, WOKING

York - Mount Hermon Roads

Vicar: The Revd. J.E. Marshall, M.A.

HANDEL'S

MESSIAH

Saturday, 29th March, 1952

at 7.45 p.m.

Augmented Choir and Orchestra

Soloists:

Vera Meek — Soprano
Gwen Tingley — Contralto
Francis Hilliger — Tenor
Sydney Dixon — Bass

Fred. H. Lawes — Leader of Orchestra

Henry Doughty — Organist & Choirmaster

Clement Meek, F.R.C.O. — CONDUCTOR

ST. MARY OF BETHANY, MOUNT HERMON. - Chapel-of-ease to Christ Church. Dep.-Warden, Mr. C. E. Watkins, Carnoustie, York.Rd. Verger, Mr. G. Beale, 60, Royal Oak Rd. Services: Sundays, 8 a.m. Holy Communion; 11, Morning Service (Holy Communion. 2nd and 4th Sundays), 3 p.m. (Young People), 6.30, Evening Service (Holy Communion. 3rd Sunday). Holy Days, Holy Communion at 11.30. Baptisms, every Sunday at 4 p.m. Churchings, after any service. Hymn Book, "Church Hymns" (latest edition)

KINGSWAY CHURCH ROOM (in connection with Christ Church parish). - Sundays: Sunday School, 10 and 3. Thurdays: Mission Service, 8.15 p.m., etc. Hon. Treasurer, Mr. C. E. Watkins.

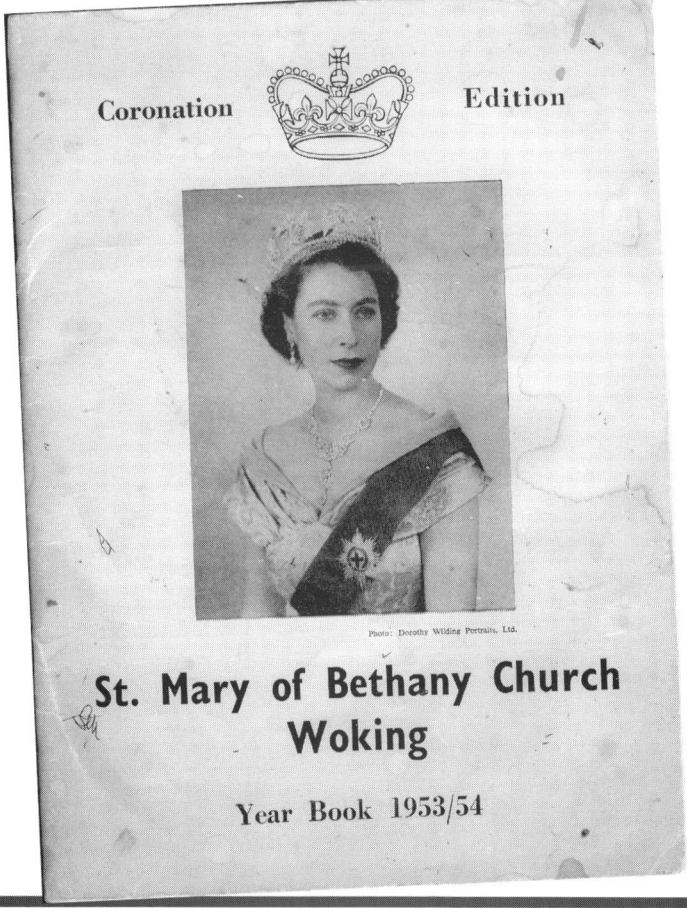

Woking Directory 1919.
Local Memoranda Section.
Details of local Churches.

Coronation Year Book 1953.

This photograph was taken on 17th October 1956 on the 50th anniversary of the laying of the foundation stone. The group was photographed on the stage in the Kingsway Hall. A great deal of effort was obviously spent in getting together all these clergy. Parties were very formal in the 1950's!

The photograph shows Miss C Hamilton, the daughter of Rev WFT Hamilton, 2 previous vicars of St Marys - Rev J E Marshall and his wife, Rev S W Phillips and his wife and the then current vicar Rev R M Brettell. The vicar of Christ Church, Rev W H Read and the preceding vicar Rev J C Banham who by then had been promoted to Canon. The Rev A C B Bellerby was a retired clergyman. The Christ Church clergy are represented because Christ Church is St Marys patron.

Diagram of the changes proposed to the paths including retaining walls by the new porch and a new path around the north side.

On the wall are two partially hidden posters. The one on the right says *'Woking Crusade'* and the left one advertises *'The Woking Area Association of The Church Missionary Society'* holding an evening event in October.

Around 150 parishioners were present. Constance Hamilton recalled laying the foundation stone and being present with her brother Herbert at the dedication of the church.

A Jubilee Gift Day raised £314 which was earmarked for resurfacing the paths and building a new path around the north side of the church.

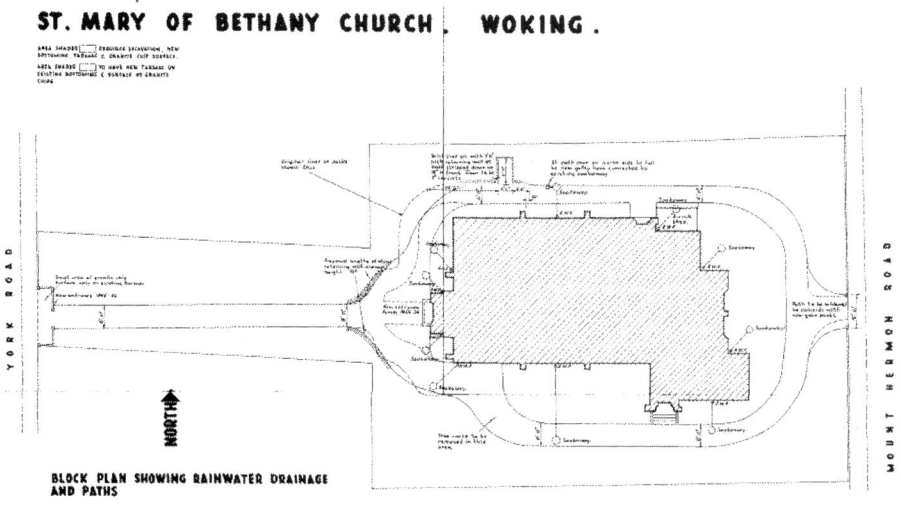

ST. MARY OF BETHANY CHURCH, WOKING.

BLOCK PLAN SHOWING RAINWATER DRAINAGE AND PATHS

Rev ACB Bellerby MA   Rev WH Read MA   Rev RM Brettell MA   Rev SW Phillips MA
Vicar of Christ Church 1953-   *Vicar 1953-*   *Vicar 1924-1944*

Rev J E Marshall   Mrs J E Marshall   Miss C Hamilton   Mrs S W Phillips   Canon JC Banham MA
Vicar 1945-1953   *Vicar of Christ Church 1928-1952*

SYDNEY FRANCIS, A.I.B.P., A.R.P.S.
Phone: Woking 1391.
for
Woking News & Mail
Phone: Woking 2821.

46400/39A

This is stamped on the reverse of the photograph. Sydney Francis was probably Woking's best known photographer.

Diary for the beginning of Lent 1933. Note the novel way for clearing the deficit. A half-crown or 2/6d is 12½p.

Parish of St. Mary of Bethany, Woking.

Vicar: REV. STANLEY W. PHILLIPS, M.A.
Wardens : Mr. M. G. NOLL, and Mr. R. B. ROBERTS
Parochial Treasurer : Mr. A S. WHITBURN,
Elmcroft, Claremont Avenue

CHURCH SERVICES

Feb. 19—Quinquagesima
  8 a.m. Holy Communion
  11 a.m. Morning Prayer
  3 p.m. Young People's Service
  6.30 p.m. Evening Prayer & Holy Communion
  Preacher—M. & E. : The Vicar
Collections : Church Expenses

Ash Wednesday, Feb. 22—
  8 a.m. Holy Communion
  3 p.m. Litany and Address   Prebendary Hinde

Friday, Feb. 24—St. Matthias' Day
  12.0 Holy Communion

Feb. 26—1st Sunday in Lent
  8 a.m. Holy Communion
  11 a.m. Morning Prayer & Holy Communion
  3 p.m. Young People's Service
  6.30 p.m. Evening Prayer
  Preachers—M. : The Very Rev. Dean Mayers
      E. : The Vicar
Collections : Vicar's Stipend Fund

Wednesday, Mar. 1—
  Day of Prayer for our own Parish
  8.0 a.m. Holy Communion
  12.0 }
  3.0   } Short Services of Intercession
  8.15 }
      Preacher at 3 p.m.—Rev. H. P. Walkden

Friday, Mar. 3—12.0 Holy Communion

Mar. 5—2nd Sunday in Lent
  7 a.m. Holy Communion
  8 a.m. Holy Communion (Young People)
  11 a.m. Morning Prayer
  3 p.m. Young People's Service
  6.30 p.m. Evening Prayer
  Preacher—M. & E. : The Vicar
Collections : Special Half-Crown Fund

Some other regular Engagements

Sundays—3 p.m. Young Women's Bible-Class, at Stoneleigh
Mondays—5.15 p.m. Kingsway Y.P.U.   7 p.m. Scouts
Tuesdays—12-12.30 Provident Club
    5.15 p.m. Wolf-Cubs
Wednesdays—2.30 p.m. Mothers' Fellowship
Thursdays—8 p.m. Full Choir Practice
Fridays—5.15 p.m. Mt. Hermon Y.P.U.
    8.30 p.m. Girl Guides
    6.30 p.m. Prayer-Meeting in the Vestry
Saturdays—2.30 to 4 p.m. Brownies

Also—

**Wednesday, Feb. 22nd — Kingsway Hall Prayer
Meeting**

Friday, Feb. 24th—**"The Jew in a Changing World"
Rally for Young People** in Central Y.W.C.A.,
at 6.30 p.m. Speakers : Rev. L. G. M. Sheldon,
Norman Gee, &c.

Saturday, Feb. 25th—10.30 a.m. **Magazine distribution in
the Vestry**

Monday, Feb. 27th—3 p.m. **Mothers' Union** in Kingsway
Hall. Speaker : Mrs. Walkden

Day of Prayer for the Parish

8 a.m. Holy Communion. Prayer for our Country
12.0   Prayer for our Church Services, the Parochial
    Church Council, Wardens & Treasurers, the Choir,
    the life and witness here of all who bear the name
    of Christ.
3 p.m. Prayers for the homes of our parish, the Mothers'
    Union and Mothers' Fellowship, the District Visitors
    and all other workers, the magazine.
8.15 p.m. Prayer for all Young Life Work and Bible-Classes,
    the Clubs. our Sunday-Schools, the Children's Ser-
    vices, Scouts & Guides, Scripture Union, Y.P.U.

SPECIAL APPEAL FOR 1,400 HALF-CROWNS
to clear off the debt of £173/7/6 on our GENERAL PAROCHIAL FUND

Single half-crowns will be most gratefully received, and it is hoped that many will give in tens, twenties, forties, &c.
Please take one of the special Lent Self-Denial Boxes for this Fund

St Marys, as most churches, had a choir. An excellent choir affiliated to the Royal School of Church Music. It was invited to deputise for the holidaying cathedral choir at Guildford Cathedral on Sunday 12th April 1964 to lead the morning service. This was followed by deputising in 1965, 1969 & 1980. One Saturday outing in 1981 saw the choir lead worship at St Edmundsbury Cathedral, Bury St Edmunds in Suffolk. The day included lunch on the cathedral green followed by practice and the 4pm sung Evensong.

The 1980's saw a gradual change to using modern songs in worship. I can remember singing with a small group (we called ourselves Celebration) of five with one guitar. Three of us were still choir members and robed. We would come forward to the chancel steps and the other two from the nave and we would sing songs from *Living Waters*, many of them written by The Fisher Folk. The reaction to this style of music was very mixed as can be imagined. A number of people left St Marys around this time because they felt that progress towards modern styles of worship was to slow. The choir continued, eventually becoming unrobed, and then disbanded completely.

With the arrival of reordering came a new pattern of worship leading. A more 'flexible' (that is, willing to sing many styles of music) group of singers was formed with an ad hoc orchestra made up of instrumentalists who were available. These were mostly young people who were given an opportunity to take part in an activity they enjoyed. The numbers rose to about forty at it's peak.

Along came another change. The single morning service was trying to serve the needs of a traditional congregation and young families who were by now used to informal worship in other churches or who had no church background at all. It was thought that we could not meet the needs of everyone with one style of worship. The one 10am service was replaced in April 1997 with two services; a more formal liturgical service at 9.30am and a family orientated informal service at 11am. The singers and orchestra were disbanded as not being flexible enough to lead the 11am service and most did not by then want to return to traditional liturgical worship. From this grew small music groups similar in make up to pop groups with guitars, keyboards, drums etc. This change was thought very heavy handed and another group left the church for pastures new. A large number of churches around the country have also gone through these, sometimes painful, changes over a similar period.

Both Sides Of The Bridges

The 1970 choir in the car park.

1 Peter Dimmock	11 P Threadgold	20 G Snook
2 Chris Hinkins	12 Mildred Brooks	21 Trevor Worsfold
3 Peter Worsfold	13 M Bridger	22 Robert Innes
4 Richard Langtree	14 G Tyler	23 Brian Worsfold
5 F Collier	15 F Brown	24 Kevin Curling
6 David Hughes	16 Connie Green	25 R Baker
7 Trevor Cobley	17 S Brooks	26 M Richards
8 Brice Marchant	18 Diana Rawlings	27 N Collier
9 Mark Dennis	19 Pam Sleet	28 K Richards
10 John Brooks		29 N Curling
		30 Graham Worsfold

Also in the photo are, in the back row, from left to right:-
A) John Bednall *Church Warden,*
B) Rev Dale Oldham *Curate,*
C) Cyril Pawley *Choirmaster/Organist,*
D) Rev Raymond Lee *Vicar*

Not in Photo
Richard Bednall *treble*   P Richards *treble*
Eileen Bednall *soprano*   Christine Sherwell *soprano*
Catherine Lahey - Bean *soprano*

Elsie Newell recalls that she and her husband soon joined the choir after starting to attend St Marys in 1932 and became involved in other work in the church.

"My husband kept in touch with the choir boys and took them on their annual outing, whilst I assisted with the Sunday morning crèche, the church cleaning and flowers. and the music. We had a very good choir and for many years won the shield for the best choir of the year at the Churches Music Festival. During this time we were invited to sing Handel's Messiah at St George's Chapel, Windsor. As we were leaving after the Saturday rehearsal we met two ladies wearing head scarves who had been standing, outside listening. They told me how beautiful it had sounded and that it was like angels singing. They chatted to us, and I only found out later that I had been talking to Queen Elizabeth, who became the Queen Mother, and the then Princess Elizabeth, now our Queen. The following Sunday we performed the Messiah in their presence. It was a great thrill for all who took part".

Henry Doughty choirmaster remarked in a St Marys magazine:-

"Unlike so many organs which grunt, whistle, moan and, sometimes, refuse to let forth a murmur, our good tempered two manual organ only occasionally produces a rattle. Although not very resourceful it is comfortable to manage, with it's pneumatic action, and adequate for accompanying the services".

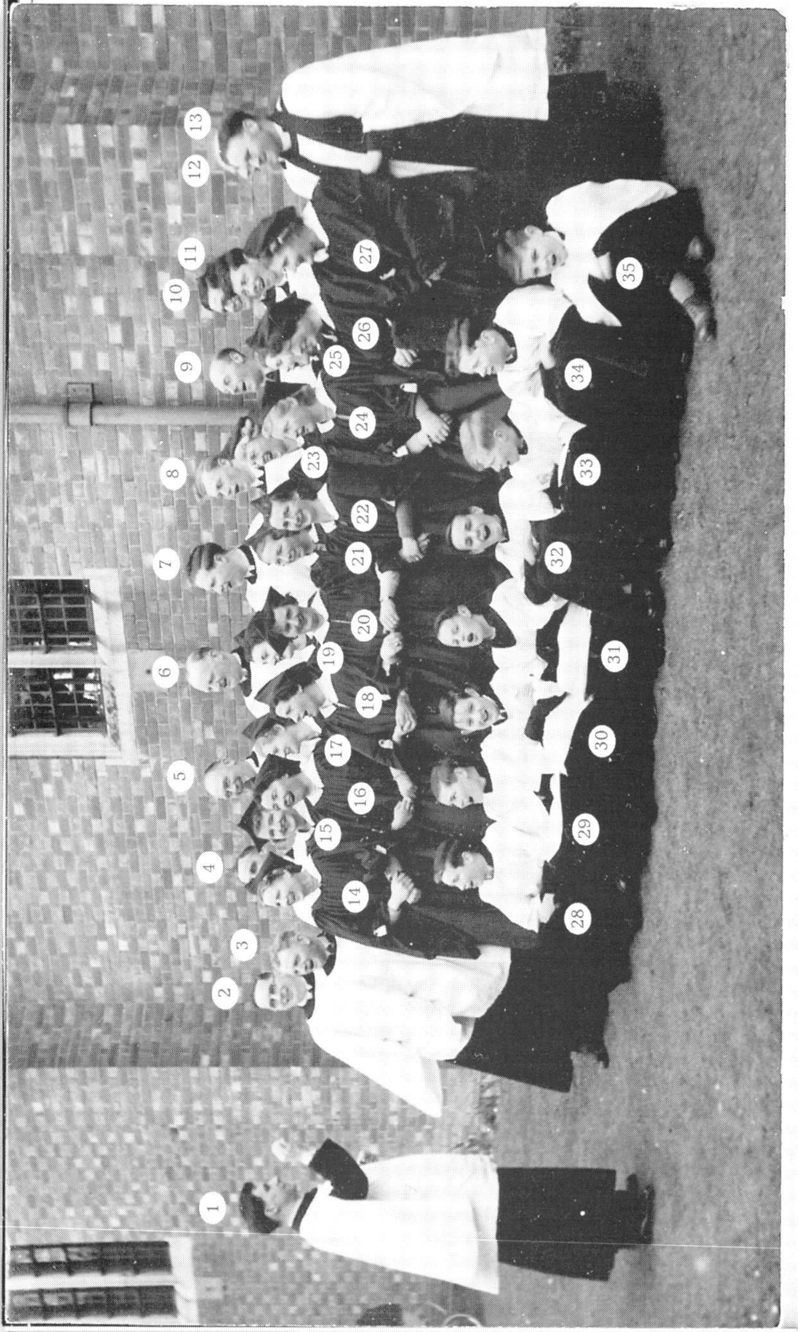

This photograph was taken on the lawn where the Hamilton Memorial Hall now stands. The Senior Choir Member, Miss Green, not shown, was one of the first women in the choir.

28 J Lawrence
29 M Robbins
30 C Goulding
31 K West
32 B Smithers
33 M Munday
34 S Colloff
35 G Smithers

14 Mrs Emily Rowne
15 Miss Claire Steer
16 Miss Muriel Martin
17 Miss Joan Jerred (Worsfold)
18 Miss Mary Drewett
19 Miss Pam Sleet
20 Mrs Vera Meek
21 Miss Jean Cook (Davis)
22 Mrs Freda Page
23 Mrs Doris Worsfold
24 Miss Betty Hall
25 Mrs Mildred Brooks
26 Miss pearl Wakefield
27 Mrs Flo Brown

1 Henry Doughty
2 Leslie Page
3 Peter Dimmock
4 Walter Lawrence
5 Fred Colson
6 Cecil Hall
7 Phillip Davis
8 Peter Worsfold
9 Arthur Worsfold
10 Lawrie Bayliss
11 Peter Colson
12 Clement Meek
13 Jack Marshall

The boys choir stalls, on the right, were added in 1926. When installed the end panels were the same height as the stalls behind. These were reduced in height in 1956 to give a more balanced look and to prevent the boys from being hidden from view.

Both Sides Of The Bridges

Choir Outing Southsea c1935 - 1939

The choir would usually organise and provide the entertainment at the New Year social and have an annual outing.

Flo Brown
Percy Brown
Mary Drewitt Connie Green
Freda Page
Laurie West? Claire Steer
Leslie Page
Elsie Newell

Rev Phillips   Muriel Martin
Arthur Worsfold   ?   Reenie Davis   Doris Worsfold
?

Arthur Worsfold, the grandfather of Graham Worsfold ran the Post Office in Mayford and would walk to St Marys twice on Sundays.

The choir boys of St Marys, Christ Church and St Pauls had their own separate outing. They were provided with a New Years party on February 15th 1924 and were entertained by a conjuror engaged for the evening from London.

This list is not quite complete. In earlier years there was often a choirmaster and organist and sometimes there were deputies as well.

Mr H C Rowntree 1907
Mr Lyon Ryde for 14 years
Mr Vincent ? -1932
Mr Lyon Ryde 1932-1933
Mr Maw 1933-1934
Mr Laurence Conway West 1934-1937
Mr Basil Pearce 1937-1940
Mr Godsland 1940- ?
Mr Henry Doughty 1945-54
Mr H Curran 1956-1958
Mr Cyril D Pawley 1959-1981
Mrs Linda van Peborgh /
        Mrs Anne Methold 1981-1985
Mrs Daphne Evans 1985-1987
Miss Merion Powell 1987-1989
Mr Philip Comley 1990-2000
Rev Steve Beak 2001 - 2005

Mr Rowntree was appointed headmaster of Church Street School Old Woking in 1906.

Mr West was the son of the founder of Conway West garage in Guildford Road and Conway West coaches of Ottershaw. After leaving Woking County School for Boys he trained to be a professional organist and played at Sutton Green and Ripley churches. He was assistant organist at St George's Chapel Windsor and then organist at the Royal Chapel in the Great Park. In 1969 he helped to launch the prestigious Windsor Festival of music.

Mr Doughty left St Marys and went to Harrow-on-the-Hill then to Truro Cathedral, where he was organist for many years playing what is accepted to be the best cathedral organ in the country. Although not playing the organ now he is still involved with music and is vice president of the Cornwall County Music Festival.

Mr Ryde's son, Humphrey, sang in the choir making a fourth generation of Rydes to worship at St Marys at 1957.

Merion Powell left St Marys to take up an appointment as repetiteur with Brussels Opera.

Mothers Union A Brief History

Mary Sumner.

The Mother' Union was started in the village of Old Alresford near Winchester in 1876 by Mary Sumner *née* Heywood (1828-1921), the wife of George Sumner, the Rector of the parish. Her own experience of motherhood made her aware of how little preparation and support women received for their vital role as mothers. This led her to invite some 30 or 40 local mothers to discuss the possibility of meeting regularly in order to help one another create a nurturing home environment in which their children could develop both physically and spiritually. Mary Sumner believed that many of society's problems could be solved if mothers were educated in the best ways of child-rearing. Prayer and practical action were at the heart of this union of mothers. Each member was given a card on which were printed simple practical suggestions for child training and the Mothers' Union Prayer.

The St Mary of Bethany branch of Mothers Union started in 1925. The banner which still hangs in the chancel was given by Mrs Frech.

The certificate shown here was presented to May Evans (the author's grandmother) on April 26th 1925. She was one of the founding members. The certificate incorporates *The Objects, The Mothers Union Prayer, Acknowledgements* to the effect that you are married, your children have been baptised, you will receive

These Term Cards are for the war years 1941-4. The note at the bottom of each card states:-

NOTE - Owing to Wartime conditions it is not possible to arrange speakers some time before the meetings. Speakers will be invited near the time of the meetings, and their names will be announced in Church.

Holy Communion and promises: *I will endeavour...*

A notebook dated 1946 has a cover made from a piece of a map folded inside out, presumably due to wartime paper shortages. Throughout the war years the MU carried on as usual with meetings, speakers, teas, bring and buy sales etc. MU met in the Kingsway Hall until the Hamilton Hall was built. Membership grew until around 1960 it stood at 69 but by 1972 it had dropped to 29.

In 1969 Raymond Lee, the vicar, was asking whether MU, Young Wives and Women's Fellowship should amalgamate to make a larger more viable group.

The certificate states:-
Diocese: Winchester
Branch: St Mary of Bethany Woking
Enrolling Member: Mary B Phillips
        (the wife of the vicar)
Admitted by: Stanley W Phillips
Members Signature: May Evans
Date: April 20th 1925.

Membership Certificate The chain border represents Mothers Union branches around the world.

The 50th anniversary of St Mary's MU was marked with a Woking Deanery Festival service at St Marys on 25th March 1975. The address was given by The Bishop of Guildford. In April 1985 the 60th anniversary was celebrated with Mrs May Evans as the last living founder member.

In the early 1980's The St Mary of Bethany MU was incorporated into the Christ Church branch. Sadly the Christ Church MU branch also closed down in the 1990's. The MU was run in a very   formal way, almost as a business, with a committee, minutes and audited accounts. It appeared from annual reports to struggle to recruit new members. Those left at the end were young mothers when they joined but left as grandmothers and great grandmothers. Why was recruiting so difficult? Did MU in the 1960's seem old fashioned and formal? Mothers Union is still strong today with 3.6 million members around the world.

Mothers Union banner which hung in the sanctuary.

This photo was taken in the summer of 1964. It was a Women's Fellowship outing to Bower Cottage Greatham, the home of (23) Anne Randall , daughter of (22) Monica Sowdon who ran the fellowship. (21) is Anne Randall's baby. (10) Mrs Champion was caretaker of the Kingsway Hall and a Sunday School teacher.

Women's Fellowship 1964.

Back Row	Centre Row	Front Row
1.	11.	18. Nancy Richardson
2.	12.	19.
3.	13.	20.
4.	14. Mabel Hutchins	21. ? Randall
5.	15.	22. Monica Sowden
6.	16.	23. Anne Randall
7.	17.	
8.		
9.		
10. Mrs Champion		

Below are names of some who
may be in the photograph

Mrs Lawrence	Mrs Kitty Martin	Mrs Seaman	Elsie Newell
Mrs Haines	Joan Thisleton	Mrs Mair	Mrs Whitemore
Edna Cobley	Mrs Anscombe	Mrs Haines	Mrs Francis
Mrs Norman	Janet Lee		

Top Gear began in 1965 when young Christians expressed concern about the failure of the churches to touch many young people so obviously at a loss for purpose in life. Churches and church youth groups had no appeal for them. Christians obviously had to go out to them. But how? Representatives of 17 local churches met to consider the question. A committee was appointed. Prayer and planning followed.

The first idea, explained the Rev. Raymond Lee, chairman of the committee, was for an early summer 1966 mission in the disused Methodist church in Commercial Road. But almost overnight the church was demolished, and effort in Woking was being heavily committed to the Billy Graham campaign. An ideally sited ware-house was made available behind Christ Church.

An appeal through Woking churches raised more than the £500 needed, water heaters, coffee machines, chairs and other equipment. A circle of 1,500 prayer partners was built up. At a preview for local church youth groups the appeal was made for "Young Evangelists" to work in the bar. Over 100 were present at the training classes that followed and they committed themselves to be at Top Gear on various evenings until the mission closed. Posters and car stickers went out. Beat groups were organised through Musical Gospel Outreach. Visits were made to youth groups and senior schools to explain the mission. And the hard work of transforming a derelict, overgrown, rubbish littered, warehouse into a with-it coffee bar was pushed forward. There was an average attendance each night from 5th - 22nd October of 700 young people. Following up those who had expressed an interest was later determined to have been poor.

In October 1968 a second Top Gear was organised in Wadham Stringer's old showroom in Commercial Road. Follow up was improved with a scheme called "Overdrive".

Top Gear logo

Rev Raymond Lee with David Methold (in light jumper) and Anne Martin, later to marry David.

Both Sides Of The Bridges

CAMEO

CAMEO - Come and Meet Each Other. This has been one of the most successful groups set up at St Marys. CAMEO was formed to meet a growing need of somewhere for over 50's to meet. Meetings are held on Thursday mornings with a format of coffee and a speaker. Occasionally lunches and outings are held. Cameo started in 1983 with Ken and Peggy Methold as leaders. Peter and Joan Worsfold took over in 1988.

Bethany Babes

Another successful group is Bethany Babes a mother and toddler group staffed by St Mary's members. It started in 1984 with a Monday afternoon session and has grown to four sessions a week. This has become a valued meeting place for parents and carers with under school age children

Scouts & Guides

On 1st August 1907 Lord Robert Baden-Powell opened his experimental camp on Brownsea Island for 20 boys. This is agreed to be the day when Scouting was founded, and so 1st August 2007 was celebrated as the birthday of Scouting with special events worldwide. Since 1907 almost half a billion young people all over the world have pledged to live by the Scout Promise and Law. The Scout Association (UK) was closely involved with these celebrations.

The 7th Woking Scout group was founded in 1925 a year after St Marys became a separate parish. It has always been a very strong group both in numbers and achievement. Today it is the largest group in Woking. The group now includes Cub Scouts and Beavers. The Guide group is 6th Woking and includes Brownies & Rainbows.

All of these groups are affiliated to St Marys.

Youth Fellowship

The Youth Fellowship, Young Peoples Fellowship or Young Christians Fellowship, remembering some of the titles, was started in 1948 by the vicar Jack Marshall. There had been youth clubs before which mainly concentrated on sport and pastimes. This new venture held on the second and fourth Sunday evenings of each month in the Kingsway Hall was organised by and for the youth of St Marys.

Today, it seems almost incomprehensible that a church like St Marys could be without house groups or cell groups, such is the recognition of their importance in the social and spiritual life of the church. Back in the 1940's and 1950's, however, the only available opportunities for people to relate to one another on a personal basis were through joining the choir, the Mother's Union or the weekly bible study prayer meetings. Things began to change in the 1950's when a group of "20 and 30 year olds" from several of the local churches - St Mary of Bethany, St Johns and Holy Trinity Knaphill - started meeting together in each others' homes for study and discussion. The only other House Meetings during this period were those run by Dr. Jack Simmonds who had returned from the mission field in Uganda to practice locally in Woking. It was really not until Raymond Lee came in 1962, that positive encouragement was given for lay people to hold such meetings and the foundations were laid for the house church structure that we know today.

Prior to the building of the Hamilton Memorial Hall most of the children's work at St Marys centred on the Kingsway Hall. In the 1940's the Sunday School was

A Sunday School class in the Kingsway Hall garden C1951.

well attended as relatively few parents owned cars during and after the war so there were far fewer competing activities for children. It is therefore no surprise that the Summer Outings proved very popular. The numbers attending the Sunday Schools were such that it was necessary to hire three or four coaches to take all the children and teachers for their "annual outing by the sea". In those days, the Sunday School at the Kingsway Hall covered the full age range. The formidable Sunday School Superintendent, Miss Daisy Wright, was equipped with a large hand bell which she rang for silence - and she got it!

The original "Sunday School" concept of having all the age groups together, gave way in the 1960's to separate the youth work in the church into "Climbers", "Explorers", "Pathfinders" and the "Youth Fellowship" (and for a time) in the 1960's, a "20 to 30" age group.

Both Sides Of The Bridges

Unfortunately not all magazines were kept for posterity. The first one, when St Marys became a separate parish, has been kept along with April 1931, 4 incomplete bound volumes from Dec 1943 to Dec 1958 Mar/April 1984- Aug/Sep 1989 and a few other odd copies exist..

November 1965
"A new FAMILY SERVICE every Sunday at 10 a.m. began on Harvest Festival Sunday, 3rd October. It was attended by over 500 people, a record attendance at any service ever held in our church on a Sunday. On the following Sunday (which was not a festival) there was an attendance of 270, almost three times the number of those who have been attending Morning Prayer at 11 in recent months. It is quite clear that this service is one the most likely to grow and attract newcomers, as has already happened at Pyrford and St. John's."

November 1963
Rosemary Richardson lent her sheep *Shonny* to the vicarage to reduce the tough bits of grass to normal height.

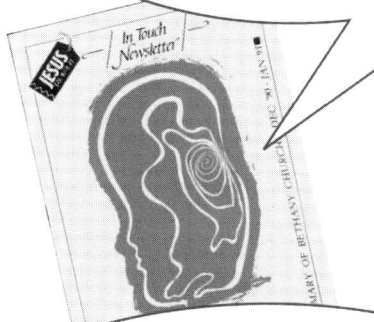

February 1959
"The St. Mary of Bethany Cubs (7th Woking) have recently obtained a new colour which will be dedicated on February 1st, at 11a.m. At the January Sunday School Service the old colour was carried for the last time by Richard Langtree. By a strange coincidence this flag was carried for the first time by his father Frank Langtree when he was a cub in the same company." (c1926)

January 1971
saw the Woking Salvation Army Corps without a home as the Halls were compulsory purchased under the town development scheme. Temporary accommodation was kindly made available in the St. Mary of Bethany Church Hall - then in the Kingsway.

Magazines have always been an integral part of church life. St Marys is no exception. Not only are they an excellent way to keep people informed but they also make church members feel more a part of a community, and of course supply a source of material for researchers..

The St Marys magazine has taken many forms over the years. The earlier magazines were published monthly; professionally printed on coated paper usually with a diocesan monthly newsletter bound in. With the advent of church offices and duplicators these became produced in house. The results were not as good,

The first magazine

January 1956 Jubilee year magazine cover.

having been typed and then duplicated but the information was more up to date, the quantities could be varied quickly and the cost was lower. Photocopiers replaced duplicators and the quality improved. With the advent of computers, Word Processing and Desktop Publishing, weekly bulletins incorporated with service sheets are produced to a much higher quality. It is much quicker to produce one-off posters, handbills etc to publicise specific events. The internet is once again producing changes with news now available on-line and via e-mail. Information is expected more quickly these days.

The monthly magazine is probably a thing of the past.

Daphne du Maurier was born in London Author of Frenchman's Creek, Jamaica Inn and Rebecca

Probation of Offenders Act passed

Alan Wainwright was born. He wrote many books on fell walking in The Lake District He devised the now famous **Coast to Coast** walk from St Bees in Cumbria across to Robin Hood bay in Yorkshire

The Playhouse and The Queens theatres opened in London

Imperial College of Science and Technology was established by Royal Charter granted by King Edward VH on the 8th July

Lutetium (LU) an element in the Periodic Table was discovered by G. Urbain of Paris

10 men and 1 woman were **hanged for murder in** the **UK**

The first **Metered Taxi Cabs ran** in London

The Limited Partnership Act was passed

Ernest **Shackleton** led his first expedition to Antarctica on the *Nimrod*

Sir Arthur Conan Doyle wrote *The Croxley Master* and *Waterloo*

Stainer & Bell publishers of printed music and books was established

Since 1790 debates had taken place concerning the utilisation of the **metric system.** 2 debates in 1907 failed

The Breguet-Richer Gyroplane No. 1 with four bi-plane rotors powered by a 40 hp Antoinette engine carried a man into the air for 40 seconds. However, the machine had to be 'tethered' by four men to keep it stable, but this was still recorded as the **first manned ' helicopter' flight.**

Barracks at the rear of the **National Gallery** were cleared and work began on constructing five new galleries.

First Domestic **Vacuum Cleaner** invented by James Spangler & William   Hoover

First Synthetic Plastic -**Bakelite -** invented by Leo Baekland
Maria **Montessori** opened her first school and daycare centre in Rome

Rudyard Kipling won the Nobel Prize for Literature

Oklahoma became the 46th state of The United States of America.

Louis Lumiere invented colour photography.

Katharine Hepburn was born.

Ben Hur was the year's most popular film.

The Hague Conference extended the rules of war and international arbitration procedures.

Brooklands, the world's first purpose-built motor- racing circuit was constructed and opened including The Clubhouse which is now the main entrance building to Brooklands Museum.

S.F. Edge took Brooklands **first World Record** driving 1,581 miles in 24 hours

The Great Race car rally from Peking (now Beijing) to Paris.

The Queen's great grandfather King Edward VII commanded that the Automobile Club of Great Britain & Ireland should be known as the **Royal Automobile Club.**

Lord Robert Baden-Powell opened his experimental camp on Brownsea Island for 20 boys on 1st August.

Motorcycle racing around the famous **Tourist Trophy** mountain circuit on the Isle of Man started.

British Federation of Women Graduates was founded to promote the interests of women graduates world-wide.

St. Catherine's School, Bramley destroyed by fireball lightning on 11th April.

Hampstead Garden Suburb designed by Parker and Unwin, Lutyens.

Students have been learning their craft at the **Royal Horticultural Society Garden Wisley** since 1907. Wisley was purchased in 1903 by Sir Thomas Hanbury a former council member from George Fergusson Wilson and presented it to the Society as a new experimental garden

Edvard Hagerup Grieg, (1843-1907), Norwegian composer and pianist died 4th Sept , born Bergen, descended from an Aberdonian. Alexander Greig, who left Scotland in 1746.

The current **Old Bailey** was opened on the site of Newgate Prison

Both Sides Of The Bridges

Daphne Evans neè Richardson with school class in Valpariso Chile.

Raymond and Janet Lee with Joan Hall.

Top Gear.

Garden Party Invitation.

The Parish Church of
ST. MARY OF BETHANY, WOKING

The Vicar and Mrs. R. J. Lee and their children wish to invite .

to the

MISSIONARY GARDEN PARTY

in the

Vicarage Garden
(corner of York Road and Wych Hill Lane)

on

Saturday, 11th July, 1964
2.30 to 5.30 p.m.

Stalls for Cakes, Preserves, Holiday Wear, Flowers
TEAS   SIDESHOWS   ICE CREAM

Entrance: Adults 6d, Children 3d

Things have changed a huge amount in the past 100 years, for the church in this country. Back in 1907, church attendance was relatively high, community was strong, and the country's perspective on life was broadly Christian, even when people didn't go to church. As we go into our second century as a church community, we are facing a very different scenario. National attendance at church has dropped sharply over the decades, although the latest figures suggest that we have turned the corner. We are also in what might be described as a 'post-Christian' era, where much of our nation does not share our faith or Christian perspective. Here in Woking, many people have no real local community – they work elsewhere and community is through networks of work and leisure, rather than where we live.

Despite these things, we are thankful to God that we remain a growing, flourishing community of faith, seeking to love Jesus and serve others in his name. Our challenge is to maintain strong Christian community, to keep growing spiritually as Christians, and to be fruitful in mission. We are confident that, with God's help, we will continue to do that. As a parish church we are committed to meeting the hugely varying needs of a multi-generational and multi-cultural community. With a membership of around 400 adults and children, we range in age from 0 – 90+, and come from over 20 different nationalities. Our growing ministry team reflects this diversity, and we have five different styles of worship most Sundays to match different ways of connecting with God, from children's and youth congregations to very traditional worship. We also have a huge variety of small groups for fellowship and discipleship, including young people's cell groups, a learning disability group, men's and women's fellowship groups, many evening and various daytime groups. With relatively large numbers in the church as a whole, these small groups within the church are where real community is found, meeting midweek and then coming together in larger congregations for teaching and worship on Sundays.

As well as our 'in-house' activities, we are involved in local schools, residential homes, a neighbourhood care scheme, and in different aspects of general pastoral community work, reaching out with the love of Christ to those around us. We also support God's work of mission globally as well as locally, through our mission partners working in many parts of the world.

In these ways we continue to play our part in introducing people to the love, forgiveness, and power of Jesus, and by helping people to follow Him in their daily lives. All of this is in His name and for His glory – and we're so privileged to be a part of the adventure of building the Kingdom of God!

Steve Beak, July 2007.

Acknowledgements

St Mary of Bethany church for many records and photographs

Rev Raymond Lee for his foresight in bringing together from many sources old magazines, photographs and memories to form a collection of historical records.

Church members and ex members for their memories and loan of records, photographs and magazines

Surrey History Centre for many resources

Malvern College

Trinity College Cambridge

Stephen Rabson P & O History and Archives at the National Maritime Museum

The British Library

Cromer Museum

The Commonwealth Wargraves Commission

Woking History Society

National Monuments Record - English Heritage Swindon for W D Caröe's drawings & photograph of angels

Michael Langtree for his expertise in searching family records.

Woking Library for Woking News and Mail microfilm

Rushworth and Dreaper for their records.

Birmingham University Library special collection for Church Missionary Society records

Lambeth Palace Library - Church of England Records

Ordnance Survey

A History of Woking
  Alan Crosby
  Phillimore 1st edition 1982 & 2nd edition 2003

For the Family Sake
A History of the Mothers Union 1876-1975
  Olive Parker
  Mowbrays 1975

Christ Church, Woking "The Church in the Centre"
- a Centenary History
  Peter Wichmann 1993

The Origins of Christ Church Woking A Short History
  F R Amos 1977*

W D Caröe Rsto FSA: His Architectural Achievement
  Jennifer M Freeman
  Manchester University Press 1990

A Cambridge Movement
  J C Pollock
  John Murray 1953

The Olivestob Hamiltons
  Rev Arthur Wentworth Hamilton Eaton 1893

History of St Mary of Bethany Church
  Miss Leslie Wright
  unpublished 1967

The Locke Kings of Brooklands Weybridge
  J S L Pulford
  Walton & Weybridge Local History Society 1996

Twenty Years in Woking
  Woking News and Mail Feb 20th 1914
  Supplement celebrating the 1,000th issue

London's Lost Route to Basingstoke
  Story of the Basingstoke Canal
  P A L Vine
  David and Charles 1st Edition 1968

*Some material for this book was gleaned from Robert Amos's book. He had heard about Rev Raymond Lee's great interest in the history of St Mary of Bethany church and his foresight in putting together a folder of many unique documents. In this folder there are letters from Robert Amos, Christ Church PCC secretary, requesting and thanking Dr David Hughes, St Marys churchwarden, for the use of the folder in his research for his book! Raymond Lee presented the folder to St Mary of Bethany churchwardens on his departure in 1970.

Contacts

If you would like to know more about who we are and what we do please contact us.

St Mary of Bethany website
www.stmaryofbethany.org.uk

St Mary of Bethany youth website
www.smobyouth.co.uk

Church office
01483 723424
office@stmaryofbethany.org.uk

Vicar: Steve Beak
01483 761269

St Mary of Bethany
Mount Hermon Road
Woking
GU22 7UH